WTS
MOTORSTVUK

Touring Cars

Touring Cars

John Tipler

PARRAGON

First published in Great Britain in 1997 by
Parragon
13-17 Avonbridge Trading Estate
Atlantic Road, Avonmouth
Bristol BS11 9QD

ISBN: 0-75252-234-5

Conceived, designed and produced by
Brown Packaging Books Ltd
Bradley's Close
74/77 White Lion Street
London N1 9PF

Editor: Graham McColl
Designer: Colin Hawes

Printed in Italy

Picture Acknowledgements
Sutton Motorsport Images: pages 2-3, 15, 16, 17, 19,
21, 22, 23, 24, 25t, 25b, 26, 27t, 27b, 29, 30, 31, 33,
34, 35, 37, 38, 39, 40, 41, 42, 43, 44, 46, 47, 48, 49,
50, 51, 52, 53, 54, 56, 57, 58, 59t, 60, 62, 63, 64, 65,
66t, 66b, 67t, 67b, 68t, 68b, 69t, 69b, 70t, 70b, 71t,
71b, 72, 73, 74l, 74r, 75l, 75r, 76t, 76b, 77l, 77r, 78t,
78b, 79l, 79r, 80t, 80b, 81, 82l, 82r, 83l, 83r, 84l, 84r,
85l, 85r, 86t, 87l, 87r, 88l, 88r, 88-9, 89t, 90l, 90r, 91t,
91b, 92l, 92r, 93t, 93b, 94t, 94b.

Phipps Photographic: pages 6, 7, 8, 9, 10, 11, 12, 13, 14.

LAT Photographic: pages 36, 45, 55, 59b, 86b.

Contents

The History of Touring Car Racing

Beginning in the post-war years, Touring Car racing quickly grew into one of the most exhilarating categories on the competition calendar, and some of the most memorable duels on British circuits were fought out by saloon car protagonists.

Touring cars are saloon cars by another name. They shouldn't be confused with Grand Tourers such as the Aston Martin DB7 or with other GT cars such as the Porsche 911s and Ferrari F40s of this world – which have a much more exalted pedigree even though they are equally dramatically modified for racing. Touring Car racers are, externally at any rate, the same mass-produced vehicles as you find in the dealers' showrooms. Stock Car racing in the USA meant just that: they were cars taken out of the dealer's stock – and then seriously tweaked to make them handle and perform like race cars.

'Tin-top' racing, as the Touring Car form is known, became popular for several reasons. Spectators could identify with the car they drove to work or the shops every day. Also, the inter-class competition of years gone by threw up all kinds of David-and-Goliath confrontations, and a more recent phenomenon is that, because the drivers are much better protected than open-wheel racers,

Five-times 3000cc-class winner Gordon Spice heads the field in his Capri at the 1982 British GP meeting at Brands Hatch.

A typical mid-1960s duel as Chris Craft's Superspeed Anglia holds off a drifting Mini Cooper at Silverstone in 1966.

'door-handling' confrontations are inevitable and frequent. Touring Cars are excellent TV as well, with in-car cameras monitoring the action.

Over the years, there have been various championships for every kind of saloon car, from the most highly modified, like the Super Saloon silhouette cars of the mid-1970s which gave the world the Skoda-Chevrolet, to the current Class 1 World Touring Cars from Alfa, Mercedes and Opel.

Each country has its own brand of Touring Car racing, although it has become much more homogenised in Europe in the last 20 years and looks like becoming even more so, although each country continues to run its own national series.

In the Beginning

Touring – or saloon – cars were always more prominent in postwar rallying, but it was not the case on the race circuit. But the launch of the 160km/h (100mph) Mk VII Jaguar saloon in 1950 gave race fans a serious production car to cheer. Jaguar soon became the most prominent Touring Car manufacturer in the world.

In Britain, Touring Car racing has been around since the early 1950s, when club racers took to the circuits in

Touring Cars

their Mk VII Jaguars, Jowett Jupiters, Morris Minors, Rileys, Ford Populars and Austin A30s. Members of the 750 Motor Club could even be seen racing their pre-war Austin 7s. They were pitted against sports cars of the time like Healeys, MGs and XK120s, which were usually quicker and better-handling, so it became necessary to segregate them into a separate category.

Very soon, this was further broken down into classes defined by engine size, and eventually, according to degrees of modification. The first national all-saloon race was in May 1952, when the *Daily Express* sponsored the 'Production Touring Car Race' as a curtain raiser at its annual Formula 1 and 500cc event at Silverstone. It was won by Stirling Moss in the works-entered Jaguar Mk VII – a car which had also been campaigned in the RAC and Monte Carlo Rallies. Moss repeated the Silverstone win the following year in the same car.

Before long, saloon car dices were sufficiently popular for the national clubs and promoters to stage more serious events. At the 1954 *Daily Express* International meeting, the heroes of the hour – Tony Rolt, Ian Appleyard and Stirling Moss – jumped into their Jaguar

American horsepower told when Dan Gurney blasted past the predominant Jaguar Mk IIs in his Chevrolet Impala at Silverstone in 1961 – until a wheel came off.

Mk VII saloons for an entertaining thrash, with Daimler Conquest Centuries vying with Lancia Aurelia and Riley 2.5 in the 3.0-litre class. In the up-to-2.0-litre class it was Ford Consul against Borgward, and Morris Minors battled it out with Standard Eight, D.K.W. Renault 4CV and Dyna Panhard at the back of the field.

Smart Modifications

Tuning or 'hotting-up' was in its infancy, but in 1955 most runners were modifying engines and suspension systems; Ken Wharton's Ford Zephyr, for example, used a light alloy cylinder head, twin exhaust and carburettors, stiffer springs, and a racing-style bucket seat. Jaguar recruit Ivor Bueb won the 1956 Silverstone event.

Traditionalists bemoaned the tuning up of what they saw as production cars, and in 1957 regulations were tightened up, with fewer mods permitted. Jaguar still held sway, with Mike Hawthorn giving the new 3.4-engined car a debut victory at Silverstone. This continued to be Britain's most prestigious saloon car race – the Grand Prix relied on a sports car race to get things moving. At flag fall drivers sprinted across the track to jump in their cars just like contemporary Le Mans starts.

The first British Saloon Car Championship was held in 1958, with four engine-capacity classes. Round one was the 1957 Brands Hatch Boxing Day meeting. This was to be the first of a string of victories for a private Jaguar

team, Equipe Endeavour. Drivers Tommy Sopwith and Sir Gawaine Baillie were the victors. The series also took in Goodwood and Aintree, and, twice, Silverstone, where it was support race for the Grand Prix. Gone was the Le Mans-type start, with seat belts also coming into use. This event was won by American legend Walt Hansgen in one of John Coombs' Jaguars. But the first British Saloon Car Champion was Jack Sears in an Austin A105 Westminster, clinching the title by winning a tie-break race with Sopwith in a pair of identical Riley 1.5s.

There was a similar state of affairs in 1959, when Jeff Uren took the title through consistent class wins with his Ford Zephyr, in spite of Jaguar's overall supremacy. In 1960 the winning drivers were Roy Salvadori and Colin Chapman – the Lotus boss having a one-off outing – in Coombs' Mk II Jaguars, and Sears and Baillie in Sopwith's similar cars. Eventually though, the title was taken by Doc Shepherd in a highly modified Austin A40. 1961 saw the Peter Berry team running Jaguars for Bruce McLaren, John Surtees and Dennis Taylor, but they failed to match Salvadori or Mike Parkes and Graham Hill in the Sopwith team cars. The writing was on the wall for Jaguar for the first time at the 1961 *Daily Express* Silverstone meeting, as Dan Gurney out-dragged the

During the 1970 series Frank Gardner won all but one of the races he entered in the thundering TransAm 302 Boss Mustang, missing out on the title through tyre trouble in the Tourist Trophy.

Jags with his monster Chevrolet Impala. Although Hill's Mk II closed under braking and in the corners, cubic inches told on the straight. Gurney might easily have won had he not lost a wheel.

As well as winning the F1 World Championship in 1962, Graham Hill was also top scorer for Jaguar. The smaller classes were dominated by Austin A40s, Ford Anglias, Riley 1.5s, the ubiquitous Minis and, for the first time, Mini Coopers. Driving one of John Cooper's cars, John Love was outright British champion in 1962. Sir John Whitmore was runner-up the following year in a works Mini Cooper, beaten to the title by the gargantuan Ford Galaxie of Jack Sears.

Mini Magic

It was the Minis in their hordes that really captured the imagination of the general public, as they swarmed all over the big boys in the twisty bits. Also to be found at big events like the 1962 Motor 6-Hours at Brands Hatch

Lotus works driver Pete Arundell cocks a wheel of his Mk I Cortina at the Goodwood chicane, 1966.

MILESTONES

1950: Launch of the Mk VII Jaguar, first 'super touring' car

1952: The *Daily Express* sponsors the 'Production Touring Car Race' at Silverstone – won by Stirling Moss in a Jaguar

1957: Regulations tightened up by the RAC to preclude highly tuned cars

1961: Advent of US big bangers as Dan Gurney leads the Jaguars at the Silverstone meeting

1963: European Touring Car Championship inaugurated

1968: BTCC comes under jurisdiction of the RAC.

1970: Regulations revert to Group 2 specification

1985: All-powerful Ford Sierra ushers in turbo era

1990: BTCC refined to two-class structure. Robb Gravett provides Cossie swansong

1991: One-class BTCC launched; Will Hoy is champion in a BMW M3

1992: BTCC comes under TOCA management to become top-line travelling circus

1995: FIA coins term 'Super Touring' for Class 2 saloons

1996: Frank Biela is the BTCC's first four-wheel drive champion with an Audi A4

were Sunbeam Rapiers, Vauxhall VX4/90s and Alfa Romeo Giuliettas, but the front runners were in Mk II Jaguars. As much as anything, this event was the big Jag's swansong; although it was won by Parkes/Blumer, the Mini Cooper of Denny Hulme/John Aley was third – after six hours' racing. As well as being a manufacturer of roll-over bars, Aley was a key promoter of the European Touring Car championship, which got going in 1963. Victor of the inaugural series was Peter Nocker in a 3.8 Jaguar Mk II.

Scene Stealers

In Britain the Jaguars were still in contention at the head of the field, but now the top drivers like Sears and Baillie were getting into Galaxies and winning as they pleased. At the first of two Brands Hatch six hour marathons, it was Jim Clark's turn to trounce the Jaguars, while at the second meeting two Grand Prix stars – Dan Gurney and Jack Brabham – and all-round ace John Sprinzel were Galaxie mounted. But it poured with rain, leaving the big American Fords foundering hopelessly. And now, waiting in the wings were smaller Fords – Cortinas this time, built by Lotus.

In 1964, the Mini Cooper assault on the Touring Car scene was double-edged. Ken Tyrrell entered two cars for Warwick Banks and Julian Vernaeve in the embryonic European series, while John Fitzpatrick drove for John Cooper in British events. Such was the devastating impact of the Mini Cooper on the continent that Banks took the European title outright. Fitzpatrick, meanwhile, managed second overall and took the 1300cc class win in the domestic series. The Mini's reputation as a giant-killer lasted more than 10 years. In Mini-Se7en form it comprised the first of the one-make championships that mushroomed in the 1980s – from Renault 5 to Eurocar Sierra. In its heyday it competed in endurance races like the Spa 24-Hours.

Family Car Racers

The notion of a family saloon as racing car was down to Ford's Walter Hayes, who commissioned Lotus to build the Lotus Cortina using Ford's new 1500cc block with a

The 3.0-litre Capris and BMWs, which are seen here in pursuit at the Silverstone TT in 1976, possessed greater reliability than Jaguar's 5.3-litre XJ12 Coupés, which were were fast but fragile.

Touring Cars

Lotus twin-cam head. The cars were assembled at Lotus's Cheshunt factory, with coil spring rear suspension instead of leaf springs, and on occasion they were tested by Colin Chapman himself. The works cars' international debut was at Oulton Park in 1963, in the hands of Jack Sears and Trevor Taylor, where they beat all the Jaguars. Lotus had two Lotus Cortina teams, one contesting the British and European championships, and the other concentrating on American events. No less than 27 drivers were signed up, including Jim Clark, who two-wheeled his way to the British title in 1964.

Engine size told the following year, as Roy Pierpoint won with a Mustang. By now the Lotus Cortinas had reverted to leaf-spring rear suspension, and Sir John Whitmore won the European Touring Car series in one of the red-and-gold Alan Mann-entered cars – Whitmore

Andy Rouse's battered Broadspeed Capri attacks John Fitzpatrick's works' Cologne Capri at Silverstone during the 1973 Tourist Trophy.

was relaxed enough to wave to spectators in the heat of the race. He faced stiff opposition too, from the newly formed works-backed Autodelta Alfa Romeo team. Led by Andrea de Adamich driving lightweight Giulia GTAs, the Alfa squad boasted the services of Jochen Rindt on occasion. Alfa won the European series in 1966, with De Adamich the champion.

Regulations in Britain were now tightened up – Group 5 superseded Group 2 – and national Champion in 1966 was John Fitzpatrick, former Mini and Fiat Abarth racer, winning in a 1.0-litre Broadspeed Anglia.

Big Bangers

Over in the States, the equivalent series was the TransAm, the province of the home-grown Mustang and Camaro. Alfa GTAs and Lotus Cortinas did well there, with Horst Kwech taking the 2.0-litre class honours in a GTA. In Britain in 1967, the big American V8 was the machine to have in order to be in contention. Mustangs were fashionable, but Aussie Frank Gardner rediscovered

the ex-1963 Monte Carlo Rally Ford Falcons, and, with a bit of preparation, swept all before him in the red-and-gold Alan Mann Falcon. His main challenger was fellow Aussie Brian Muir in the John Willment Galaxie. The 1.0-litre category was consistently won by John Fitzpatrick in the Broadspeed Anglia, with Cooper Ss of Rhodes and John Handley dominant in the next size up.

Other contenders normally associated with the Grand Touring category and rallying slipped into the European Touring Car frame in 1968. The 2.0-litre Porsche 911S was now a leading challenger, with the occasional Jolly Club Lancia Fulvia thrown in against the 1300 Giulia GTA Juniors. BMW 2002s matched the new supercharged Giulia GT SAs, with the odd Mustang in the leading bunch. It was an exciting time, with new manufacturers popping up and Grand Prix stars still showing off their skills in saloons. Nowadays the BTCC is a refuge for GP drivers whose career in F1 has come to an end; they can blossom anew in touring cars.

Now under the jurisdiction of the RAC's Motor Sports Authority, the British Touring Car scene in 1968 came to be dominated by Frank Gardner, first in Alan Mann's Mk II Cortina-Lotus, then in the new Escort. Ford did much the same with its Escort as it had done with the Cortina. A twin-cam engine ensured its homologation as a race car and once again there was little the rest could do to stop Gardner in the Alan Mann car.

Alec Poole took the 1969 Championship with the Arden Mini, and then for 1970 motor racing's governing body, the FIA, revised the rules, reverting to a clearer specification for Group 2 cars which excluded cars like the Porsche 911.

Gardner's weapon for the 1970 British and European series was a TransAm Mustang 302. This thundering beast won every time out, apart from when tyre troubles lost it the Tourist Trophy, a glitch which cost Frank the title. Nevertheless, for several seasons he held more British lap records than any other driver.

Gardner's Boss Mustang was written off by Australian dockers in the winter lay-off when it dropped from a crane and plummeted on to the dockside from a great

Car-wars were in full swing in 1963, and BMW's weapon was the awesome 3.0 CSL 'Batmobile', driven here by Dutch legend Toine Hezemans.

height. For 1971 he drove the SCA Freight Chevrolet Camaro Z28. There were some nail-biting duels with the similar Wiggins Teape-sponsored Camaro of Brian Muir, when either one could win. Present-day Classic Touring Car racing pits examples of these great cars from the halcyon days against each other once again.

As the Escort developed into a sophisticated racing car, powered by 2.0-litre Cosworth BDA engines, drivers like Fitzpatrick and Dave Brodie were able to challenge the 5.7-litre Camaros of Gardner and Muir. But at the 1971 Motor Show 200-saloon classic at Brands Hatch, Gerry Birrell scored a lucky win in his Capri as Gardner and Fitzpatrick collided and destroyed their cars against a bridge parapet on the last lap.

In Britain it was much the same story in 1972, with Gardner's Camaro regularly cleaning up, but the consistency of Bill McGovern paid off for title honours for the third year running with his 1.0-litre Bevan Imp.

Car Wars

On the continent a major scrap was brewing between the big 3.0 BMWs and the Ford Cologne 3.0 Capris. The action was characterized by the close racing at Paul Ricard circuit, with Jackie Stewart/Francois Cevert – among other leading lights – in factory and privately run Capris door-handling with works models, Alpina and

Touring Cars

Alfetta GTV heads a Jaguar XJ12 Coupé and Chevrolet Camaro at Silverstone during the 1976 Tourist Trophy.

Schnitzer BMW CSL coupés. In the mid-field category, Dave Matthews/Andy Rouse beat the BMWs in their Broadspeed Escort.

At season's end Jochen Mass was champion driver in a works Capri, but the Alfa GTA Junior was still dominant in the 1300cc class, taking the manufacturers' title through most class wins, while Alfa GT Ams swapped paint with BMW 2002Tiis in the 2.0-litre category. Bizarrely, the big Capris and BMWs were also eligible for World Sportscar events this year, racing against sports prototypes at Le Mans.

By 1973 the mainstream championships had become so expensive to compete in that privateers virtually disappeared. Sponsorship or a factory contract was vital. The might of Ford Koln failed to match the lightweight BMWs that year, aerofoils sprouting from the bootlids earning them the 'Batmobile' nickname. The V6 Capris couldn't live with them. Apart from the BMWs' wings, all modified touring cars had bulging wheel arches and chin spoilers by now, growing larger with each passing season to accommodate ever-widening tyres.

In Britain, regulations switched to virtually standard Group 1 cars for a couple of years as a cost-saving exercise. BMW was promoting itself heavily in Britain, but rally star Roger Clark's team of Alfa Romeo GTVs won the BMW Raceday at Brands Hatch. John Handley and Stan Clark also won the Manufacturers' Award for Alfa in the 1973 Tour of Britain. In the Tourist Trophy at Silverstone, Derek Bell/Harald Ertl won for BMW Alpina after a sterling drive by Jochen Mass in a Capri RS. Overall, the Escorts were sufficiently fast and numerous to pip Alfa for the title by one point.

With big BMWs competing with Opel Commodores and the odd Capri for race wins, the Alfa 2000 GTVs continued to dominate Class 2 in Europe during 1974 and 1975. By 1976, the Alfetta GTV was taking its place with equal success. This model was developed into the GTV6, providing the mainstay of mid-field action well into the mid-1980s. Indeed, Andy Rouse was British champion in 1983 in a GTV6.

Back in 1974, another Imp racer, Bernard Unett, took the title with the Sunbeam Avenger, while Andy Rouse scored the first of his string of championship victories in 1975 with a Triumph Dolomite Sprint. Motor sport tends to be episodic, with one model head-and-shoulders above the rest for a while, and the Dolomite was probably the best British touring car of the mid-1970s. Big American cars were excluded after the earlier rule changes but Richard Lloyd and Stuart Graham revived the Camaro's successes in 1974 and 1975. The TransAm car's European equivalent was the Ford Capri. No-one put it to better use than Gordon Spice. He won the 3000cc class five times from 1976 to 1980.

Jaguar reared its head again in 1976 and 1977 with the 5.3-litre XJ12 Coupé, which proved fast but unreliable even in the capable hands of Rouse, Fitzpatrick and Derek Bell. Top ETC scorer in 1976 was Pierre Dieudonné with a BMW 3.2 CSL, with Dieter Quester European champ in 1977 in a similar car.

While the big guns squabbled for race wins, Unett made off with the British Championship the next two years running in the Avenger. In 1978 and 1979, Mini tuning-ace Richard Longman was top dog with his 1275 Mini GT, then stalwart all-rounder Win Percy took us into the 1980s with two consecutive championships with the TWR Mazda RX-7, capturing a third title in 1982 with the Toyota GB Corolla.

Big Cats Pounce Back

Jaguar reappeared on the European scene in 1982 with the V12 XJ-S, and Tom Walkinshaw's TWR team won the Brno GP, Nürburgring and Silverstone TT that year. Walkinshaw narrowly missed the ETC title in 1983, but made sure of it in 1984 with a string of impressive victories, including the Spa 24 Hours, against the big BMWs, notably those of Quester, Kelleners and Stuck. Jaguar withdrew, leaving TWR to concentrate on racing the aged 3.5-litre Rover SD1. These cars had been dominant in their class in the early 1980s.

Andy Rouse followed his Alfa GTV6 success of 1983 with two victories in 1984 and 1985, driving a self-prepared Rover SD1 Vitesse and Ford

Sierra Turbo. This was the turbo era; on the European stage the Volvo 242T with traction control was surprisingly successful, with Renault 5 Maxi-Turbo and 21 supreme in France, and the Alfa 75 Turbo in Italy.

In Britain, be-winged Sierra Cosworths began their indomitable rise. Despite their amazing 500bhp, a current BTCC car is faster around Brands with only 300bhp, proving what a handful RS500 Sierras were to drive. Although Rouse was top Cossie scorer in 1986, there were eight different winners at the 12 rounds in 1987. By virtue of consistent class wins, Chris Hodgetts was champ in 1986 and 1987 in the Toyota GB Corolla.

Turbocharged Triumphs

The RS500 Sierra Cosworth and the BMW M3 were built-to-race homologation specials. Although they ran in different classes they could vie with one another for championship honours. Another old hand, Frank Sytner, showed what the turbocharged M3 could do in 1988 by taking 11 class wins and giving BMW its first British Championship. John Cleland scored for Vauxhall Dealer Sport with the 16-valve Astra GTE the following year.

The touring car formula was refined in 1990 to a two-class structure; up to and above 2.0 litres. Gravett provided the Sierra Cosworth's swansong, with nine victories, while Cleland halted Sytner's – and BMW's – winning streak with the new Vauxhall Cavalier. This gave us an excellent introduction to the new BTCC with its one-class 2.0-litre limit, launched in 1991.

By 1990 the Sierra Cosworth's days were numbered in the BTCC, and here, Tim Harvey gives his RS500 a final airing at a damp midsummer Oulton Park.

The Advent of Super Touring

The 1990s saw Touring Car racing become acknowledged as the most consistently competitive form of saloon car racing. Now known as Super Touring, its special brand of close racing attracts the major manufacturers as well as millions of devoted fans.

The current era of Touring Car racing in Britain began with the 1991 BTCC. Gone were Group A supercars like the RS500 Sierra Cosworth. In came the 2.0-litre, single-class formula. This tempted many major manufacturers to participate, through existing racing teams and dedicated dealerships, and intense rivalry ensued. BMW, Vauxhall, Toyota, Ford, Mitsubishi and Nissan were represented.

It was a huge success in terms of close racing and pitting front-wheel drive against traditional rear-wheel drive; also entered, occasionally, were four-wheel drive cars like Dave Brodie's 4x4 Sapphire. The title went right down to the wire with the rear-drive Vic Lee Motorsport-run BMW M3 of Will Hoy just pipping John Cleland's front-drive works Vauxhall Cavalier. The series was sponsored by Esso, and of the 15 rounds in 1991, eight were won by rear-wheel drive and seven by front-drive cars, although a weight penalty prevented the BMWs being totally dominant. They had to carry some 99kg (220lb) ballast to counter their rear-drive advantage.

Yellow peril: Renault Laguna twins Menu and Hoy lead the pack down to Donington's Redgate corner in the opening round of the 1996 BTCC.

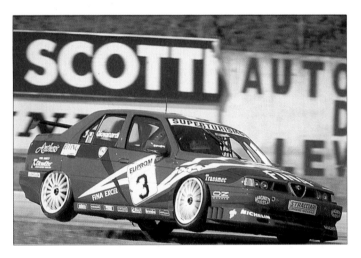

Fabrizio Giovanardi's Alfa 155 rides the kerbs at Binetto during round 4 of the 1996 Italian Superturismo series.

Qualifying now actually meant that what you saw on the grid was what it seemed, as in single-seater formulae, rather than a mixture of cars from different classes who would be struggling for class points as much as overall success. Drivers from different backgrounds contested the series. As well as tin-top specialists like Andy Rouse, Steve Soper and Jeff Allam, there were Formula 1 stars like Jonathan Palmer and Julian Bailey, who were joined by Will Hoy and Ray Bellm from the world of Le Mans-type Group C sports racing cars.

In 1991 the dominant team was VLM, Vic Lee's private venture. VLM was sponsored by Securicor and Listerine, and their cars' BMW engines were prepared by Mike Jordan's Eurotech firm in Coventry. They proved faster in a straight line than rival BMWs. Part of Vic Lee's success was the choice of Yokohama and, latterly, Toyo tyres, which lasted better than Pirelli and Dunlop at the time. This ensured that drivers Hoy and Bellm were regularly front-runners, and Hoy got off the mark quickly with wins in the first couple of rounds.

The works BMWs were entrusted to Prodrive, with Jonathan Palmer, Steve Soper and Tim Sugden at the helm. It was a new venture for the ex-F1 ace, and it

SPORTING REGULATIONS

The *Auto Trader* RAC British Touring Car Championship meetings – to give the BTCC its full title – have international status and are run according to the general regulations of the RAC Motor Sport Authority as well as the series' own rules, which in turn incorporate the FIA's Super Touring Technical Regulations. Any racing driver with an appropriate International Racing Licence can take part.

Race format
- Each race is over a minimum of 60km (38 miles)
- Wherever possible races are over 75km (46 miles)
- All BTCC events run to the two-race format with at least 90 minutes in between. This regime allows any damage or settings compromised in the earlier event to be attended to
- At the British Grand Prix support race, held at Silverstone in July, one BTCC event is on Saturday and the other on Sunday
- Start of the first race is generally between noon and 12.30pm, with the second between 3.00 and 3.30pm

Qualifying
- Qualifying normally consists of two 30-minute practice sessions at each meeting
- There is a break of two hours between
- Times set during first practice allocate the grid positions for Race 1
- Times from the second session count for Race 2
- Drivers must complete at least three laps in qualifying to start the race
- Drivers who fail to do this can still start from the back of the grid, provided they have set a time in the other qualifying session
- An untimed warm-up session lasting 15 minutes is held on race-day morning
- An untimed practice period of 15 minutes is usually held on the morning of official qualifying
- In addition to any private testing, TOCA stages two official test days at each circuit on the BTCC calendar in the run-up to the meeting
- Apart from on test days, no practising is allowed on a particular circuit until after all its scheduled championship rounds are completed

took him several races to get on top of things but by the penultimate round he had achieved one pole position. The Prodrive M3s were shod with Pirelli rubber, and this proved their Achilles heel as the tyres 'went off' after a few laps in hot weather. As it was, Tim Sugden scored once at a cool Brands Hatch in June, while Soper won three times while 'on vacation' from Germany.

Cleland's Dunlop-shod Cavalier was fast in a straight line, and stable in long sweeping bends because of its front-drive layout, but was handicapped – like all front-drivers – with torque-steer and axle-tramp 'hop' as it struggled for traction exiting corners. Things improved when he went over to radial-plys in mid-season.

The Andy Rouse-prepared Kaliber Toyota Carina finished third in the Championship, which was a real achievement for a car with absolutely no competition pedigree. It showed its potential straight away but it did not start winning until the first-ever BTCC double-round, at Donington Park in July.

Rouse used Yokohama tyres, and during the latter part of the season was the most consistent performer, although the Carina was generally not as agile a car as either the BMW M3 or the Cavalier.

The top four drivers in the championship – Will Hoy, John Cleland, Andy Rouse and Steve Soper – all won three races, although Cleland's fourth win in a rain-shortened race mid-season did not count.

Tim Harvey drove the third VLM Labatt's-sponsored BMW M3, and won the year's last race, his first that season. The Janspeed Nissan Primeras of Kieth O'dor and Julian Bailey showed promise at season's end.

The British Touring Car Championship has grown rapidly and has gained enormously in status and influence since its renaissance in 1991. It has been run since 1992 by Alan Gow's TOCA Ltd, an independent, privately owned company, which was established specifically to manage the series. TOCA (Touring Car Association) is also involved in the operation of the

Australian Super Touring series and in the North American Touring Car Championships.

TOCA Takes Over

In 1992 the BTCC, under the management of TOCA, set out to encourage new manufacturers. Having persuaded Peugeot and Mazda to get on board, TOCA added a sparkling package of support races to transform the BTCC into a top-line travelling roadshow.

For manufacturers, the stakes were raised: a good showing on the race track was reflected in a pay-off in the showroom. What developed was a win-at-any-cost attitude, which saw even more of the bumping and boring to put the man in front into the gravel trap. It was a mode of conduct which was here to stay.

It had the same effect in the BTCC results as in Germany. With Cleland out of the way, because of a controversial incident with Steve Soper, Tim Harvey's fourth place at Silverstone in the Listerine-sponsored VLM BMW gave him the title. For his part, Cleland spoke of 'the slippery slope', and the incident caused him to consider what his future tactics should be.

Vauxhall began the season strongly, with Cleland winning three of the first five events with the Yokohama-shod Cavalier GSi. He was hotly pursued for Toyota by Rouse and Hoy, who won at Oulton Park and Snetterton respectively. Hoy sat on pole no fewer than five times, and the Carinas were the quickest cars at mid-season. But the Toyota threat receded when the two Carinas collided at Brands Hatch trying to decide which was actually the quickest. Hoy bounced back to win the first part of the 'double-header' at Donington, but in the second race Harvey's VLM-run BMW just prevented a Toyota back-to-back victory.

Then it was Vauxhall's turn again, with Jeff Allam winning the race at Silverstone's British Grand Prix meeting. The BMWs were handicapped on the long straights by their rear-drive weight penalty, the engines having too much work to do compared with the

Mayhem erupts at the Nürburgring during a round of the 1996 International Touring Car Championship, as highly modified 4WD V6 Opel Calibras and Alfa 155s battle with Mercedes Benz.

Vauxhalls and Toyotas. Immediately after this race, the BMWs were allowed to drop 25kg (56lb) of their 100kg (224lb) weight penalty, and were back in contention. Both the VLM and Prodrive operations had a difficult first half of the season sorting out the new BMW 318is Coupés, with Prodrive further disadvantaged by a lack of Yokohama rubber. Although the 318is used much of the old M3's de-stroked running gear and front suspension, the new Z-axle rear end proved troublesome in race format, particularly on bumpy circuits.

Allam won the inaugural event at Knockhill. He too was prevented from landing a double by hard-charging Tim Harvey. This was the first of five consecutive triumphs for Harvey, who also scored at Pembrey, Brands – twice – and Donington.

CHAMPIONSHIP POINTS

Within the BTCC there are championships for drivers, manufacturers and teams, as well as the Total Cup for privateers (see page 28).

In the Drivers' Championship, an additional point is awarded for pole position in each round. In the event of a dead-heat at season's end, the number of race wins scored by the drivers concerned is taken into account, then second places, until a champion emerges. Drivers can score points in different cars, but may make only one change of drivetrain format – that's to say, go from front-wheel drive to four-wheel drive.

In the Manufacturers' Championship, only the highest placed car from each manufacturer can score points. So, hypothetically, a Ford which finishes fourth behind three Vauxhalls scores 12 points.

In the Team Championship, points are awarded to the two highest finishers from each team.

Each category uses the same points system:

1st: 15pts	**2nd: 12pts**
3rd: 10pts	**4th: 8pts**
5th: 6pts	**6th: 5pts**
7th: 4pts	**8th 3pts**
9th: 2pts	**10th: 1pt**

BMW domination

The Nissan Primera of Kieth O'dor, Patrick Watts' Mazda 323F and the Ecurie Ecosse ex-works Vauxhall of David Leslie made progress in the season, but Robb Gravett's Peugeot 405Mi16 struggled for most of the year. As it was, the BMW 318i eventually emerged as the pace-setter, despite Steve Soper's tendency to indulge in early-lap incidents. Harvey scored four convincing wins, taking the Championship battle to the final round at Silverstone, where Hoy and Cleland were also in with a chance. Andy Rouse's Toyota won this explosive finale, but Cleland's hopes were dashed in the controversial incident with Soper's VLM BMW, while Hoy finished fifth.

Other aspects of the season included the arrest of team principal Vic Lee on suspicion of drug smuggling (for which he was later imprisoned) and Cleland driving to third place at Donington with his torso strapped up following a testing accident. The TOCA privateer award went to James Kaye in the Park Lane Toyota Carina. Kaye narrowly beat the BMWs of Matt Neal and Sean Walker.

New Sponsor *Auto Trader* Arrives

Sponsored for the first time by every used-car buyers' favourite reading – *Auto Trader* magazine – the 1993 BTCC was also notable for Ford's comeback and for the first BTCC challenge from Renault – both of those teams gained some race wins. It was also the first year in which FISA adopted the BTCC formula for its international Touring Car category.

There was a slight upset to the form books as BTCC newcomer Jo Winkelhock had the edge over BMW sparring partner Steve Soper. The Schnitzer BMW squad staked its claim from the outset, running new four-door 318s saloons which were evolutions of the previous year's coupes, and Winkelhock and Soper won seven of the first eight races. While better-qualifying front-wheel drive cars squirmed for traction as the lights went green, the Yokohama-shod BMWs sailed sublimely into the first corner and away from the rest of the field. The late-braking German won at Donington, twice at Oulton, at Pembrey and at Brands, and established such a lead in the Championship that in the latter part of the season he was able to cruise to a certain extent.

The BMWs still ran on Yokohama tyres, but Dunlop and Michelin were making up ground. There was also a general trend for Super Touring cars to get even lower and stiffer in the suspension department, and the slightest tweaks brought about major differences in cars' behaviour. Masses of computerized information was available from the cars' on-board telemetry data-logging equipment, and as cars grew increasingly sophisticated, they handled more and more like single-seaters. So close was the competition between cars that they only had to find half a second to make the difference between being a front runner and an also-ran.

Perfecting Preparation

Setting-up became more of an art form, and team principals like Ray Mallock and Andy Rouse put their varied and extensive race experience to good use to interpret all this data. It accounted for the Ecurie Ecosse Cavaliers' and Ford Mondeos' rapid improvement.

The Mallock-prepared Ecurie Ecosse Cavaliers were putting the works' Dealersport cars to shame, and at a

mere fraction of their rivals' budget. The RouseSport-prepared V6 Ford Mondeos appeared halfway through the season, and the New Zealander Paul Radisich claimed his maiden BTCC victory – and Ford's 200th in touring cars – at Brands Hatch.

The Mondeo had a wider track than any of its rivals, and was seen to ride the kerbs better than any other front-wheel drive car. Radisich scored wins twice more and finished third in the Championship.

Tim Harvey had transferred to Renault, and he interrupted the sequence of BMW victories by winning at a rain-soaked Donington Park in the R19. Nissan,

The 1991 BTCC result went down to the wire, with Will Hoy's VLM-prepared BMW M3 – seen here in action at Silverstone — just beating John Cleland's Cavalier to the title.

Touring Cars

Vauxhall and Toyota each won a race before Winkelhock won his fifth of the year. Kieth O'dor's fine-handling but underpowered Janspeed Primera led Win Percy in a Nissan one-two at the British Grand Prix meeting, which turned out to be more notable for the amazing sight of Toyota runner Julian Bailey tipping team-mate Will Hoy into a barrel roll.

Of the rest, John Cleland was victorious on home territory at Knockhill, driving a revamped Cavalier, and Bailey also won at the Scottish track in the TOM'S Toyota Carina. Both of the French teams proved to be well off the pace for reasons of technical underdevelopment, but the Swiss Alain Menu was usually quicker in the 16-valve R19 than his Renault team-mate Harvey. Peugeot's ex-rally team struggled all season to sort out problems with the 405's chassis while the Mazda runner Patrick Watts showed a good deal of initial promise in the underfunded V6 Xedos.

The BTCC is full of thrills and spills, and in 1996 James Thompson's Mallock-prepared Vectra succumbed to the gravel trap and a close encounter with the Brands Hatch tyre barrier.

At season's end, Jo Winkelhock was the first non-British driver since 1973 to win the BTCC title, while top privateer in 1993 was Matt Neal in a BMW.

New Challengers From Sweden and Italy

An end-of-season race at Monza – the FIA (Fédération Internationale de l'Automobile) Touring Car Challenge – pointed the way forward to increased international competition and to an annual race at a different venue. It took place at Donington in 1994 and at Paul Ricard circuit in Provence in 1995. In 1996 the race was scheduled for the Salzburgring in Austria but was cancelled due to an insufficient number of entries. Back at Monza, scarlet Alfa Romeo 155TSs mixed it with the visiting BTCC circus but Paul Radisich's Mondeo was never headed. Alfa Romeo would be one of 10 manufacturers represented in the 1994 British series.

The other key player to launch an assault on the BTCC in 1994 was Volvo. After TWR spent much time testing the 850 saloon and estate back to back, Volvo elected to go with the estate – as bizarre a vision as the so-called Ferrari 250GT 'Breadvan' of 1962. As TWR predicted, 1994 was more of a learning year for the

team and
star drivers Rickard Rydell
and Jan Lammers, the estate being fast but,
unsurprisingly, something of a handful in slower corners.

However, it was the Italian team which was to steal
the spotlight with a well-planned attack, as the ex-
Formula 1 racer Gabriele Tarquini won the first five
rounds with the Michelin-shod 155TS.

At first, the BTCC paddock was outraged by the Alfa
155's apparent aerodynamic advantage gained by its
rear wing and adjustable front airdam splitter –
legitimately homologated by the FIA of course – and
when the Ford team's protest was upheld, albeit
temporarily by the RAC MSA, Alfa withdrew from the
May Oulton Park meeting. After a compromise was
reached, the Alfas rejoined the fray at Donington. From
1 July, splitters would be pushed back.

Radisich's Ford Mondeo won at Silverstone and was in
with a chance of catching Tarquini, although the
promise of the previous season had evaporated with a
string of engine problems, and he had to settle for third
in the title race. Consistency paid off: Menu ended the
season second in the points standings.

Cleland's Mallock-prepared Vauxhall entered the
reckoning after he had attained a sparkling double
victory at Donington, but Allam played strictly a
supporting role. Another two wins at Brands Hatch for
Tarquini strengthened his grip on the title. His major

**Jo Winkelhock was a newcomer to the BTCC in
1993 and, with his Schnitzer-BMW team-mate Steve
Soper, he won seven of the first eight races.**

setback of the season came at Knockhill, where Harvey
flipped him into a spectacular roll.

Winkelhock fought back into contention for BMW
following a mid-season weight review, which resulted in
rear-drive cars losing 25kg (56lb) while the rest gained
that amount. Thus the 1993 champion won four times
in the dynamically superior 318i. One of these wins was
at Silverstone at the British Grand Prix meeting, where
he was hounded by the Alfa of Tarquini sporting its
revised front splitter.

Nissan drivers Eric van der Poele and Kieth O'dor
excelled themselves by depositing their Primeras in front
of Nissan's hospitality suite at the first corner. Matt Neal's
Silverstone roll also marked the end of the Mazda Xedos
challenge, which was sadly without the benefit of
sufficient corporate funds to continue, and Neal and
Leslie were left high and dry. Now in the Peugeot team,
Patrick Watts did well in the 405, whereas team-mate
Eugene O'Brien gained the nickname 'General Accident'.
Poor aerodynamics spoiled an otherwise good car. For

Caged and belted, Giampiero Simoni awaits the start of the race in his Alfa Romeo 155 TS at Brands Hatch, 1995.

Hoy and Bailey it was to be a season-long struggle in poor-handling Carinas.

Tarquini Takes the Title
Meanwhile Tarquini continued to build up the points with high-scoring finishes while Menu emerged as the only possible title contender with a string of good performances. But second place and a win at Silverstone's double-header clinched the titles for Tarquini and Alfa Romeo. The icing on the cake was team-mate Giampiero Simoni's win in the last round of the season.

The FIA Touring Car Challenge meeting – also counting as the Tourist Trophy – at Donington in October brought, as did Monza in 1993, a decisive win for Radisich and the Mondeo. For 100km (63 miles), he held off 38 of Europe's Super Touring aces. Frank Biela's third-placed Audi 80 Quattro was punted off by Winkelhock, who claimed the Audi's brake lights weren't working. Newly crowned BTCC champ Tarquini managed fourth despite a big first-lap altercation with Cleland and Pirro's Audi 80 Quattro.

All Change
As the Schnitzer BMW and Nissan teams pulled out and Alfa Corse left its 155TSs in the capable hands of Prodrive, the new faces for 1995 were the Williams team running the Renault Lagunas, Honda Accords, and stars of the calibre of Derek Warwick, two-wheel champ Johnny Cecotto, Kelvin Burt and David Brabham.

The FIA stopped referring to Class 2 touring cars in favour of the term 'Super Touring', and there were 25 rounds for the nine manufacturers to contest.

There was a reversal of fortune in the Alfa camp. Derek Warwick and Simoni struggled with under-developed new 155s and outclassed engines; even when they drafted Tarquini back in there was no recovery. The star cars for 1995 were the Lagunas and the Volvos, with Cleland's Cavalier soldiering on.

One of touring car racing's biggest stars, Rickard Rydell, breaks open the champagne to celebrate his victory at Thruxton in August 1996.

As Volvo's star waned, so the Laguna proved to be in the ascendant; and the Renault's success turned out to be positively dramatic towards the end of the year. Menu excelled at the Oulton Park meeting, winning three out of four races there. He and Hoy filled the first two places in September to give the Lagunas their first one-two result.

The triumph was repeated at the last meeting of the season at Silverstone, as Menu took round 24 with Hoy second, and the places were reversed in round 25. Menu's tally of seven wins – one more than champion Cleland – made him runner-up in the Championship. Hoy won three times.

The reliability of the Cavalier, now in its last season, made the difference, and John Cleland claimed his

There was intense pressure from the 20-valve Volvo 850s – saloons now instead of estates – of Rickard Rydell and Tim Harvey, and as the result of a skirmish at Snetterton in August, TWR was fined a hefty £10,000 when Harvey punted out Alain Menu's Laguna in two successive races.

Rydell was on pole position 13 times, but managed just four wins and third place in the Championship, which seemed scant reward. Harvey won rounds three and four at Brands Hatch, and was second to Rydell at Knockhill and to Hoy at Snetterton.

After back-to-back testing, TWR elected to race the estate version of the Volvo 850 in 1994. Jan Lammers – here on the grid at Brands – found the car a handful in corners.

On his way to the 1994 BTCC title, Gabriele Tarquini ran away with the first five rounds in the Alfa Romeo 155 TS, including this Thruxton race.

second drivers' title almost at a canter, winning six races and scoring well in almost all the remaining rounds. The manufacturers' title fell to Renault.

The BMWs of Cecotto and Brabham had a dismal season among the privateers, never coming higher than fourth and fifth. Tyres played their part, and the fact that privateers like Nigel Smith and Matt Neal were able to get on terms with the works BMWs illustrated the importance of tyre choice. Top scorers in the Total Cup were Matt Neal, Richard Kaye and Nigel Smith.

Mercifully, serious accidents are rare in touring car racing. But there was a tragedy in the BTCC ranks when Kieth O'dor was killed at Berlin's Avus race track. He was competing for Nissan in the German *Superturenwagen* series and had already won a race that day – Nissan's first German success – and had put the year-old car on

pole for the next event. In a mid-race incident, his Primera was T-boned while stationary in the middle of the track. Sadly, he didn't stand a chance. Top Australian touring car racer Gregg Hansford had also died in a similar incident in his Mondeo at Phillip Island in March.

FIA's Touring Car Challenge bash was held in October at the Paul Ricard circuit in Provence. Present were 40 of the world's best tin-top exponents but most of the BTCC aces finished qualifying well down the rankings. It was the four-wheel drive Audi 80 Quattros of German aces Frank Biela, Hans Stuck and Italian champ Emanuele Pirro that were setting the pace. Unable to demonstrate much form in the BTCC, the BMW 318is driven at the French meeting by Steve Soper, Johnny Cecotto, Yvan Muller and Roberto Ravaglia were, strangely, the Audi's closest challengers. The reasoning was that the higher downforce aerodynamic wing settings of the majority of BTCC cars were homologated for British circuits, and they simply didn't work for the front-drive cars on the very fast Paul Ricard circuit.

In the 1990s Touring Car racing rivals Formula One for glamour both on and off the track.

The FIA World Championship

The term Super Touring was applied to Class 2 cars by the sport's governing body, FIA, in 1995 and Touring Car racing is now so widely established on the world stage that it may soon rival the Grand Prix circus in popularity. Going some way to acknowledging this, FIA introduced a World Championship for Class 1 cars in 1996. This was derived from the German Class 1 Championship and features more highly modified saloons than in the BTCC.

Like all Class 2 Super Touring cars, those competing in the *Auto Trader* RAC British Touring Car Championship are easily recognizable as mass-produced 2.0-litre, four-door family cars. They may have a lower, squatter stance and fatter wheels than normal and are covered in sponsors' logos, but they all still look more or less like their road-going siblings. But beneath those innocuous shells lie highly sophisticated racing cars. It's difficult to quantify the price of one of these cars, but in 1994 the estimated value of a RouseSport Ford Mondeo was £200,000 due to costs of development and materials.

Without exception, the cars conform to regulations which ensure that every major manufacturer has a car in its range which can be transformed into a competitive racing car. They have to comply with the international rules set up by the FIA, based on those which came into force in Britain in 1990 and designed to get as many different models racing as competitively as possible.

Enormous Television Exposure

The British public's awareness of the BTCC has been raised by BBC TV's *Grandstand*, which televised virtually every round of the BTCC from 1989 onwards. An estimated audience of over five million tunes in to watch each round, with expert commentary from Murray Walker and Charlie Cox in 1997. There are big crowds at the circuits too. In 1996 Snetterton had its biggest crowd ever – 30,000 – for the BTCC rounds 11 and 12. There

was also a magazine dedicated to the cause, entitled *Super Touring*. And as it grew in prominence, the BTCC set new standards for close racing, manufacturer participation and innovative marketing. Jonathan Gill's MPA Fingal PR firm did an excellent job on promotion.

For sponsors and manufacturers, the financial advantages are clear. A season in the BTCC might cost two million pounds for a two-car team, reckoned to be worth an estimated £250,000 in exposure time at each race. In comparison, a three-month TV ad campaign would cost perhaps £6 million, and the clincher is that the BTCC spectators are a captive audience.

It was the BTCC which spawned the 2.0-litre Super Touring class, but while remaining essentially a British series, it is generally acclaimed as the pinnacle of Super Touring racing. The BTCC's prestige and format now extends all over the world. From Germany and France, Belgium and Spain, to Czechoslovakia and Italy, Super Touring thrives, as indeed it does in Japan, South Africa, Australasia and North America, where the cars involved are in some cases different to European models. Its character is such that many international manufacturers utilize their involvement in the sport for their marketing and advertising programmes.

The big news for the BTCC in 1996 was the entry of the four-wheel drive Audi A4s of German star Frank Biela

Helped out by Audi's PR people, popular 1996 BTCC Champion Frank Biela signs autographs for fans at Brands Hatch after winning round three.

and BTCC rookie John Bintcliffe. Ranged against this untried pairing were the Schnitzer BMWs of Roberto Ravaglia and Jo Winkelhock, plus the 1995 front runners.

A Flying Start for Biela

At the Donington openers, Biela was up and away. It was the same at Brands Hatch for round three, although Winkelhock came through to win round four. The Audi pairing of Biela and Bintcliffe managed fourth and fifth here, but on to the fast sweeping expanses of Thruxton, the Audis once more looked supreme. They cleaned up round five, but round six was a different matter, with Winkelhock and Ravaglia making it a BMW one-two.

Kelvin Burt demonstrated the Volvo's speed at Silverstone, winning round seven, but the BMWs weren't far behind. As the Vauxhalls slid further back, the Hondas and Peugeots trod water in the mid-field, with the Mondeos well out of it. At Oulton Park, round nine went to Winkelhock and round 10 to Rydell in the Volvo.

By the time the circus arrived at sunny Snetterton in June the Audis were no longer the threat they had appeared to be at the beginning of the year, and this

was in some part due to the imposition of a 30kg (67lb) weight penalty. This was administered by TOCA in a bid to maintain some sort of parity between the different runners. One consequence was that Jo Winkelhock started both Snetterton races from pole, coming fifth in the first and winning the second.

The Dynamic Duo

The privateers' battle was by now down to just two remaining contestants, with Richard Kaye challenging Lee Brookes for Total Cup honours (see box below). Neither regulars Hamish Irvine nor Nigel Smith were present. Such a low level of support for the Total Cup was a poor reward for the French fuel company. In view of the general excellence of the BTCC it was very surprising that more privateers weren't attracted by it – budgets are about the same in the comparatively dull Rover Turbo Cup series.

If rounds 13 and 14 at Brands Hatch Grand Prix circuit were somewhat processional compared with the usual cut and thrust of BTCC races, they were also a double triumph for Alain Menu's Renault Laguna, with

THE TOTAL CUP

For the last four years, this category has been sponsored by the French Total petroleum company. Privately run independent teams race alongside the works-backed professionals, and as well as challenging – theoretically – for BTCC points, they qualify for Total Cup honours.

The first driver to finish in the Total Cup category scores 15 points, the second 12, and so on, as in the main Championship. Total Cup contestants who finish in the top 10 score points in the overall Drivers' Championship. Total Cup entrants are also eligible for the Teams' Championship, and prize money is generous; privateers in the Total Cup category are chasing four big cash prizes.

The Total prize money
The Total Cup winning driver gets £60,000, the runner-up £30,000, with the third-placed driver receiving £20,000. For the privateer most often

fastest in qualifying, there is also the 'Total Cup Flyer' Trophy and a £5000 cash prize.

TOCA also pays bonuses of £20,000 to privateers who contest all rounds, paid in two instalments: £10,000 following round 14 to drivers who have participated in rounds one to 14, and £10,000 at the end of the season for those who have participated in rounds 15 to 25. Total Oil GB funds a promotions package to the tune of £100,000.

Drivers or teams can go in for the Total Cup provided they own the car, or have possession of it under a normal commercial leasing arrangement. No-one is allowed to receive exclusive support from the manufacturer or importer that isn't available to any other privateer running a similar car.

The Total Cup ideal that a privateer can get in among factory runners holds true, as exemplified by Richard Kaye's sterling drives in the Mint Motorsport ex-works Cavalier during the 1996 season.

Hoy in contention too. Biela's second place in round 13 took him further ahead in the points table, but Menu's pace at Brands made him look like a potential champion.

The first half of the 1997 season was dominated by the Renault Lagunas, with Alain Menu virtually invincible and his new team-mate Jason Plato frequently a front runner. At the late May double-header at Oulton Park, Menu topped the podium twice and was way ahead in the points table. Plato lay third in the championship, behind Volvo S40 pilot Rickard Rydell. Making a welcome return to the BTCC was 1994 Champion Gabriele Tarquini, now driving a Prodrive-prepared Accord, and fourth in the title chase. Another erstwhile Alfa driver was back too: Derek Warwick, partnering John Cleland in the Vectra camp. The Audis of Biela and Bintcliffe were relieved of 30kg (66lb) of their weight penalty and, thanks in part to better Dunlops, consequently showed signs of improvement, having been midfield runners along with Leslie and Reid in the Nissans and Watts and Harvey in the Peugeots. Meanwhile, poor Radisich and new team-mate Hoy continued to be out of luck in the Mondeos.

Reigning Total Cup champ Lee Brookes was busy sorting out his ex-works Peugeot 406, while Matt Neal's Team Dynamics Mondeo was steadily improving. Robb Gravett seemed to be having some luck at last, now with the Graham Hathaway prepared Honda Accord, while newcomers Jamie Wall in the Mint Motorsport Cavalier and Colin Gallie in the Dave Cook Racing BMW 320i promised fireworks.

Battle of the privateers: the Cavalier and Carina of Total Cup protagonists Richard Kaye and Lee Brookes round Druids Hairpin at Brands Hatch in April 1996.

Touring Cars Around the World

Touring Cars come in several indigenous forms, all impressive in their own way: the States has NASCAR and TransAm, Australia has its own Bathurst-style tourers, while the Formula 1 of Super Touring is the stunningly high-tech Class 1 ITC.

TransAm and NASCAR

There are traditionally two categories of saloon car racing in North America, although Super Touring took off there in 1996. In the 1960s and 1970s, the TransAm series was the nearest equivalent to touring car racing European-style. It was organized by the Sports Car Club of America – the SCCA. This 25-race championship was very much the province of the pony cars: Mustang, Camaro, Cougar. Soon, models like the AMC Javelin and Pontiac Firebird – later actually called the TransAm – staked their claim. These rumbling V8 fastbacks also made their mark in Europe in the late 1960s, and today the TransAm series is still a key feature on the American racing calendar. Although quintessentially North American in flavour, there was a successful European invasion when the Audi 200 Turbo Quattros won the TransAm championship in 1988. The 1996 series was hotly contested by the Mustangs of Tom Kendall, Boris Said and Dorsey

Schroeder, with Scott Sharp and Ron Fellows in Camaros. Tempted by the delights of big-time USA, former GP driver and BTCC and Spanish Super Touring runner Eric van der Poele finished seventh in a Camaro at Minneapolis in July.

If the Mondeo Eurocars are the current European equivalent of the American stock car, look no further than NASCAR for their inspiration. Competitors in the National Association for Stock Car Auto Racing series, or NASCAR as it's commonly known, began in the post-war years with 'stock' sedans. These were, in theory, taken out of showroom stock – that's what the term meant. In practice, of course, it was very different, with all sorts of alterations soon being made to gain racing advantages. The category evolved in the southern states, where legend has it that the 'good ole boys' would hot up their cars more often than not in a bid to out-run those of the Highway Patrol when they were indulging in running moonshine or some other illicit activity. Very soon they were racing against each other, and a network of circuits grew up at places like Daytona, Talladega, Richmond, Atlanta, and Riverside. The 30-race Grand National championship was zealously

Former F1 World Champion Alan Jones heads Ford Falcon team mate Tony Romano at Sandown during a round of the 1996 Australian Touring Car series.

NASCAR stockers thunder round the banked North Wilksboro oval during round three of the 1996 Winston Cup series.

guarded by its coordinator Bill France and his son Bill jnr, who has been at the helm since 1971.

Cars like the Plymouth Road Runner, Dodge Charger, Pontiac GTO and Chevrolet Chevelle typified the raw material for NASCAR in the 1960s and 1970s. A decade or so later, this type of racing was brought to the silver screen with the film *Days of Thunder*, starring Tom Cruise and Nicole Kidman, and the grandstands for NASCAR's *Winston Cup* series are invariably packed out.

There are dynasties – the Pettys, the Allisons – and greats like A.J.Foyt. Both Ford and General Motors' badged marques – the Ford Thunderbird and Chevrolet Monte Carlo are current favourites – are out in force, the cars resembling their street equivalents in silhouette only. It is nothing if not spectacular, with strings of cars slipstreaming (drafting) around the banked bends at an average lap speed of 320km/h (200mph), often for 800km (500 miles) duration – which means hectic pit stops. The administrators maintain parity between competing cars by means of weight penalties, carburettor restrictors and aerodynamic adjustments, and close racing is assured by frequent caution laps in the wake of incidents. In 1995, NASCAR arrived at the Indianapolis raceway, and the inaugural meeting was won by rising talent Jeff Gordon. It looked as if NASCAR stockers had finally usurped CART and USAC single seaters in terms of popularity.

Bathurst 1000

Down under they've got one of the very best tin-top races in the world, where racing is fast and furious and lasts six hours. In-car camera techniques were pioneered here, treating panel-beating fans to a first-hand glimpse of how it feels to be nudged at 160km/h (90mph).

The Bathurst classic is currently called the Tooheys 1000 – in deference to its beer sponsor – and is staged on a famously hard, fast, steep circuit called Mount Panorama near Bathurst. It's a real occasion, as much for spectators as competitors. The 'top of the hill' becomes a virtual no-go area for the police and decent God-fearing types, as those with more cubic centimetres than sense perform drunken burn-outs and doughnuts on the circuit's campsite backroad.

The date for the Bathurst classic – Australia's most important domestic motor race – changed from Easter to October in 1974. The event goes back to Easter 1938, and its story has been episodic according to rule

changes and, broadly, the fortunes of Ford and General Motors' Holdens have ebbed and flowed accordingly. During the 1950s the Ford Zephyrs were no match for the Holden hordes, even when tuned up – the ratio was about 10 to 1. Bathurst was something of a free-for-all until the rules were tightened up in 1960. Then in 1964 the Cortina turned everything on its head, and, as in Europe, the lighter Ford could beat the heavier and more powerful Jaguar Mk II. Holden's S4 Bathurst Specials didn't get a look in, and before long there were even locally built limited-edition Cortina GT500s, specially tailored for Bathurst.

Although the Mini Cooper S was dominant in 1966, the next phase belonged to the American-style Mustang-derived Falcon GT. It was another comparatively light car, yet far more powerful than the Mini Cooper S, and lap times tumbled. Bathurst victors alternated between Ford and Holden as boardroom battles were acted out on the race track; 1967 was the year of the Ford Falcon GT, and 1968 was down to the Monaro as GM-H sought to smarten up its image. Yet during the late 1960s and up to 1972, when Allan Moffat's TransAm Mustang lost narrowly to Pete Geoghegan's Falcon GT, the Fords were pretty much supreme. Certainly Holdens were in the picture, with Bruce McPhee and Barry Mulholland's GTS Monaro 327 V8 winning the Hardie-Ferodo 500 in 1968, and Colin Bond and Tony Roberts victorious in a similar car in 1969.

From then on it was the turn of the Falcon GT in Phase I XR, Phase II XW, and its ultimate development, the now highly desirable XY Phase III GTHO. (Both Ford and Holden went in for such impenetrable model suffixes.) Aussies tend to prefer four doors, and although the late-1960s Falcon, Monaro and Charger were two-door fastbacks, the next generation was all four-door saloons. These big tourers were involved in breathtaking confrontations on Mount Panorama with the Holden Monaro HT and HGs and L34 Torana XU-1 V8s versus the Falcons, and Chrysler in there too with its E49 R/T Charger V8 muscle-car. Of the Europeans, only the Alfa Romeo Giulia coupés in the hands of John French and Kevin Bartlett could hold a candle to the mighty V8s.

The high-tech ITC field roars away from the start at Estoril in May 1996, with Alessandro Nannini's victorious Martini Racing Alfa 155 V6 heading the pack – the works Alfa won both races.

Touring Cars

A 'supercar' scare halted the power surge, briefly, and these low-volume 200-a-year production racers were no more. The rules were modified to allow modifications, so different cars came to the fore. In 1973, when the Bathurst was first run to 1000km (625 miles), Moffat and Geoghegan ran a new two-door fastback Ford Falcon XA coupé to victory. This model was a winner throughout the decade. The Torana L34 of Peter Brock and Brian Sampson won in 1975 and Bob Morris and John Fitzpatrick likewise in 1976. For 1977 Moffat and Colin Bond made it a Ford one-two with Falcon Superbirds.

Holden swept back with the A9X Torana and the 308 Commodore in the hands of Peter Brock and Jim

Champagne celebrations on the podium after the Silverstone stage of the 1996 International Touring Car Championship.

Richards to trounce the Fords in 1978. The story was much the same in 1979 and 1980. Brock's Marlboro Holden Dealer Team car set the pace, then Dick Johnson renewed Ford's success with the Falcon XD. By 1982, Holden had recovered, and Brock and Larry Perkins' Commodore led a four-car clean sweep. In 1983 Allan Moffat's ATCC-winning Mazda RX7 posed a threat, but Brock's Commodore triumphed again, hitting 285km/h (168mph) along the celebrated Conrod straight. He and Perkins won again in 1984.

The rules changed to international Group A specifications in 1985, and Ford was wrong-footed. Victory at Bathurst went to John Goss and Armin Hahne in the TWR Jaguar XJS V12 – the model's final victory. Then Holden bounced back as Alan Grice and Graeme Bailey won with a Commodore in 1986.

There followed another sea change. In 1987 Dick Johnson was the first and initially the fastest of the next generation of Ford runners, bringing the 550bhp Sierra Cosworth to Bathurst. It was an era of comprehensive domination, and in the late 1980s Sierra Cosworths ruled. The Nissan Skyline GT-Rs briefly wore the crown, but nowadays it's a two-horse race again with just the home-grown 5.0-litre V8 Ford Falcon and Holden Commodore going at it hammer and tongs.

Super Touring 2.0-litres have been in Australia for four years now, a reflection of the increasing number of European cars on the streets, and they have been mixing it with the big V8s. BTCC regulars Jeff Allam, John Cleland, Win Percy and Steve Soper, plus Kiwi Paul Radisich and German Jo Winkelhock are honorary Bathurst veterans. Former BTCC champ Frank Gardner recruited Soper, Allam and Winkelhock to bolster BMW's four-car assault in 1993. Locals going in for Super Touring are Geoff Brabham and Jim Richards, who won both Super Touring races at Adelaide with a Mondeo in November 1995. But legends like Peter Brock, Mark Skaife, F1 Champ Alan Jones and Allan Moffat are the big draws at Bathurst's six-hour marathon.

The ITC
The International Touring Car Championship was introduced by the FIA in 1996 for Class 1 vehicles, and grew out of the high-tech German DTM touring car series. In addition to 12 races in Germany and 10 elsewhere in Europe, there were rounds in Japan and Brazil to make a 26-round series. These Class 1 cars were

vastly more modified than the Class 2 Super Touring machines which contest the BTCC, and in 1996 only three manufacturers took part. They were Mercedes Benz, Opel and Alfa Romeo.

The rounds were staged in pairs at each venue, with a gap of 10 minutes between races. Grid positions for the second race were based upon the result of the earlier one. Venues ranged from converted street layouts like Helsinki to purpose-built circuits like Hockenheim, and at the tighter tracks physical contact was frequent and violent. The second ITC race at Estoril in 1996 had to be stopped because of a completely blocked track.

Mercedes raced the big C-class model, Alfa the 155 V6, and Opel the V6 Calibra. The Opels and Alfas were four-wheel-drive machines. The sophisticated specifications included double wishbone suspension all round, hydraulically cockpit-adjustable anti-roll bars, ABS brakes, power-assisted steering and, in the Opel's case, magnesium wheel carriers and titanium hubs. The Opel and Alfa had eight-piston caliper front brakes, the Mercedes six, with four at the rear in all cases.

Maximum engine capacity was 2.5-litres and six cylinders. No turbos were allowed. Even so, they produced about 500bhp. The Alfa's engine was

Sparks fly as Ellen Lohr struggles with a puncture on her Persson Motorsport Mercedes during Silverstone's 1996 ITC round.

developed in-house by Alfa Corse; the Opel's was the result of Cosworth's research. Mercedes' V6 was derived from their production V8, and developed by AMG.

The 4WD Alfa 155 used an automatic computerized six-speed gearbox, the 4WD Opel a semi-automatic computerized Williams six-speed, and the rear-wheel-drive Mercedes transmission used a six-speed sequential shift. Both Alfa and Opel had three electronically controlled diff locks, the Mercedes a mechanical lock diff with ASR traction control.

They were comparable designs, and highly competitive, but racing success incurred a weight penalty. Anyone finishing in the top five earned ballast of up to 50kg (112lb), which was shed only by coming lower than fifth.

As in Super Touring, the drivers in Class 1 ITC came from a variety of backgrounds and it was the province of Formula 1 exiles and all-rounders. In terms of sheer spectacle it was hard to beat, but the championship collapsed in political and financial turmoil at the end of the 1996 season.

The Teams

Since 1991, 13 different teams have contested the BTCC, with an average of 12 each season. While the majority are supported or run by organizations appointed by the manufacturers there is also room for privateers competing for the Total Cup.

By its very nature, touring car racing has always had the potential to excite the spectators, but since its renaissance in 1991, the BTCC has become so popular that no fewer than 10 manufacturers have recognized the potential it also possesses to entice customers into the showrooms. Their participation has guaranteed exceptionally close competition, and no doubt will in due course further the development of the cars that we drive on the road. The lessons that are learned in racing always pay dividends further down the line, even if not in such dramatic fashion as on the track.

The 13 teams that are featured in this section include recent BTCC participants who have helped to make the series into the fascinating spectacle that it is today. Most are the factory or factory-appointed teams in search of outright BTCC honours, while a handful of them are the independent operations that are run by privateers to contest the Total Cup category. For reasons of finance, these teams invariably run year-old cars – or older – but their commitment to the sport is no less serious than that of the works boys.

The works teams are run by highly experienced and charismatic racing personalities who employ top-flight engineers and race-orientated personnel. Teams like Schnitzer BMW have been around since the early 1960s, and Alfa Romeo has been a touring car rival for just as long. But more recently we have seen participation by organizations of the calibre and finesse of TWR and the Williams Grand Prix team, and everyone else has been forced to raise their game accordingly to match and mix it with such serious competitors.

The top team in 1996 was Audi Sport, thanks to Frank Biela's consistent podium finishes. When the German wasn't winning with the all-wheel drive A4, he was almost always in the points. Every dog has its day, as they say, and it was Audi's turn to be humiliated at the start of the 1997 season. The swingeing weight penalties for four-wheel drive, coupled with the progress of other teams, rendered the silver cars mere also-rans. It was now the turn of the Williams Renault-prepared Lagunas of Menu and Plato to rule the roost, with the Hondas of Thompson and Tarquini plus the new Volvo S40s of Rydell and Burt in hot pursuit.

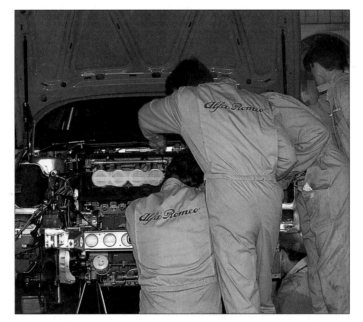

Alfa engineers swarm all over the 155's 2.0-litre twin-spark engine in the pits garage at Donington Park at the 1995 season's opener. However, Warwick and Simoni were well off the pace.

Will Hoy's Laguna sets the pace at Brands Hatch, as it hurtles down Paddock Hill Bend ahead of Kelvin Burt's Volvo, James Thompson's Vectra and Paul Radisich's Mondeo during a 1996 round.

Alfa Romeo

Having set their cars up in the Italian Superturismo series, Alfa Romeo came to the BTCC in fine shape for 1994, and Tarquini's 155 won as it pleased – until the others caught up with its aerodynamics.

Unlike most manufacturers, Alfa Romeo is steeped in competition legend, going back to its first Grand Prix car of 1914. Its BTCC contender in 1994 and 1995 was the 155, and it carried on the winning tradition of the 1960s' Giulia Sprint GTA, the 1970s' Alfetta GTV and the 75 Turbo and 3.0-litre 75 of the 1980s.

Alfa Corse – the firm's competition arm – is headed by ex-GTA racer Giorgio Pianta and design engineer Sergio Limone. They had at their disposal a budget of over £5million just to contest the BTCC. The successful 1994 contingent was managed by ex-Fiat Abarth rally star Nini

The Prodrive pit crew change the Michelins on Giampiero Simoni's 155 during a warm-up session at Brands Hatch in April 1995.

Russo with a team of 21 personnel and race engineers, including Maurizio Nardon and Steve Farrell. They had four cars at their disposal; two to race while the other two were refettled back in Turin. Engine-builders Abarth held a stock of 40 engines for 155s in various Super Touring Championships.

A Winning Team

The Alfa squad came to Britain in 1994 with fully-prepared 155s, having successfully tried the components at the firm's Balocco test track and in the Italian and German Super Touring series the previous year. They swept all before them.

The 155 was specially engineered by Alfa Corse and various specialists to comply with the FIA's Class 2 Super

Touring regulations. Thus the bodyshell is the same shape as the homologated 155 Silverstone model with its aerodynamic addenda, but its torsional rigidity benefits from being seam-welded and having a welded-in multi-tubular roll cage and suspension braces. This work is carried out by Albatech in Turin, and was so effective that the cars were initially some 40kg (88lb) under the minimum weight limit.

A First-Class Engine

Whereas the standard 155 is powered by an excellent all-alloy Alfa twin-spark engine, the racing car's engine is built for Alfa Corse by legendary Fiat-tuning experts Abarth in Turin. It is based on the cast-iron block from the 164 Turbo, and the alloy head from the 155 Q4 – the same combination as the Fiat Tipo Formula 3 motor. The head is reversed through 180 degrees to enable better engine breathing, while the internal dimensions and components are suitably re-worked using a confection of corporate parts, which still complies with the rules, to produce a square bore and stroke configuration of 86mm (3.75in).

Front-drive Super Touring cars place the majority of their weight over the front wheels – so front tyres take a real pounding under braking and in cornering – and therefore the transverse-mounted Alfa engine is canted backwards at 27 degrees to help reduce the stresses here. Peak torque is at 7000rpm, with 290bhp available at the mandatory 8500rpm limit. The 155's Brembo brakes are massive eight-pot front, four-pot rear, Le Mans class affairs, while six-speed sequential Hewland HP2000 transmissions are of Formula 1 standard. Significantly, the 155s use a hydraulic differential which can be adjusted by the driver when on the move. Speedline wheels, 21cm x 46cm (8.2in x 18in), are shod with the fast-warming Michelin tyres, so effective that Tarquini and Simoni could lead the warm-up lap at Brands Hatch as slowly as they liked yet still have the tyres at race temperature within a few hundred metres.

Bilstein dampers complement Eibach springs and MacPherson struts at the front, and fabricated-steel trailing-arm rear suspension. Trick bolt adjusters atop suspension turrets tune front camber settings. The 155 uses hydraulic power steering designed for the Lancia Delta S4 Group B rally special.

The 155's initially controversial aerodynamics of rear wing spoiler and two-position front splitter were evolved

Support teams share in all the triumphs and disasters of their drivers.

in the Fiat wind tunnel. The purpose was to eliminate lift and generate downforce, and in its initial configuration with the splitter extended, there was zero lift. When the Alfas walked away with the first round of 1994 at Thruxton, the Mondeo team protested, and the cars were withdrawn from the third round at Oulton Park. They reappeared when the rules were clarified, reputations intact, but with the front splitter retracted and rear wing extensions omitted. Gabriele Tarquini went on to win the Championship, and claimed the cars were actually improved with the revised aerodynamic settings. Another advantage the 155 always had was a relatively smooth undertray. For 1995, the rear wing became a proper racing job rather than one adapted from an Alfa 33 road car.

Political Problems

Sadly the Alfa challenge failed to materialize in 1995, when internal politics dictated Alfa Corse should hand over to Prodrive's Banbury operation. Despite the best efforts of Prodrive's Dave Benbow, Derek Warwick, Giampiero Simoni and, from mid-season, Tarquini, they were always struggling as Vauxhall, Renault and Volvo became more competitive. Tarquini claimed that the 1995 155's engine was outclassed, and a new Alfa twin-spark motor would improve the situation.

However, Alfa Romeo's fortunes continue to be very much alive in the German, Spanish and Italian Super Touring Car Championships. The chances are they will be returning to the BTCC in 1998 with the new model.

Audi

A long history of competition success with four-wheel drive models gave Audi a decisive edge in the BTCC – so much so that the cars incurred severe weight penalties in 1977

Throughout the 1996 season, one of Frank Biela's closest challengers was Alain Menu, and at Oulton Park the Laguna driver tenaciously hung on to the 4WD Audi.

The impending arrival of Audi as serious BTCC contenders in 1996 was awaited with a sense of foreboding, so dominant had their 4WD cars been in the Touring Car World Cup event at Paul Ricard. After all, it wasn't so very long ago that the Quattros had cleaned up in world class rallying.

As a manufacturer of circuit racers, Audi's involvement was historically patchy. In the late-1970s and during the 1980s, the works Audi 80s were campaigned in the European Touring Car championship by Freddy Kottulinsky, among others, and indeed Stirling Moss enjoyed a brief spell with an 80. In the late 1980s the big 200 Turbo Quattros were being campaigned by Bob Tullius's Group 44 Team in TransAm races in the USA,

and Hurley Haywood won the 1988 TransAm crown with Audi the Manufacturers' Champion. The illustrious Hans Stuck and Walter Rohrl were Audi's other drivers.

Biela Starts Winning

In Europe it wasn't until 1990 that Hans Stuck took the German title with the V8 Quattro. It was the start of a run, with new recruit Frank Biela winning the German championship in 1991. Switching to the 80 Quattro, Biela took the French touring car honours in 1993, while Emanuele Pirro won the Italian series in 1994, again with an 80 Quattro. Biela narrowly missed out to Jo Winkelhock in the 1995 German Super Touring series, but trounced everyone in the A4 Quattro in the Touring Car World Cup. Emanuele Pirro won the Italian championship once again with an A4 Quattro.

One positive factor about Audi's presence in the BTCC would be that the level of competition would inevitably be lifted to yet another high. There would, however, be a rein kept on high-tech apparatus such as the sophisticated electronic differentials, which had been highly criticized on the continent. The operation is in extremely capable hands. At the helm of Audi Sport UK is team principal Richard Lloyd, whose racing career goes back to modified sportscars – a Triumph Spitfire, in fact – in the late 1960s. He drove a Chevrolet Camaro in the British Saloon Car Championship during the early 1970s, transferring to an Opel Commodore for 1976. Richard won the 1600cc class three years running in a VW Golf GTi, setting up the specialist tuning business GTi Engineering on the strength of his success.

Lloyd first became involved with Audis in 1980, when he prepared a couple of 80s for himself and Stirling Moss to run in the British Touring Car Championship. Then he ran his own team of Porsche 924 Carrera GTs, achieving some good results with drivers like Tony Dron and Andy Rouse. For several seasons he was the leading privateer in the World Sports Prototype Championship, running the RLR Canon Racing Porsche 956, teamed with Jonathan Palmer and Jan Lammers, to eighth place

at Le Mans in 1983. In the 1985 event, Lloyd, Palmer and James Weaver finished second in the RLR 956. Many other high placings followed, with drivers of the calibre of Bob Wollek, Keke Rosberg, Derek Bell and Damon Hill piloting Lloyd's Porsche. Richard himself came out of retirement in 1993 to win the UK-based Porsche 924 Championship.

Audi Sport's team director is John Wickham, whose motor sport involvement has always been focused on team management at the highest levels. Wickham managed the Belgian RAS Volvo team in 1986, and drivers Johnny Cecótto, Anders Olofsson, Ulf Granberg and Thomas Lindström between them won seven out of 18 races in the European Touring Car series. For 1987, he set up and managed the TOM'S Toyota World Sportscar team, employing drivers like Alan Jones and Tiff Needell. Wickham then set up Footwork's F3000 team, running Damon Hill and Ukyo Katayama. He also managed the F1 team, with drivers like Warwick, Alboreto, Suzuki and Fittipaldi, when Footwork bought Arrows in 1990.

The A4 chassis are built by Audi Sport at Ingolstadt under the direction of Norbert Weber. Engine preparation is supervised by Ulrich Baretzky. The A4 is the only car in the BTCC that has a longitudinally mounted engine.

Carrying a Heavy Burden

With such a formidable management team in charge, it would be very surprising if Audi were not successful. Audi Sport chief Dr Wolfgang Ullrich once said, 'We think the BTCC is one of the most competitive championships in the world.'

That was before Audi's early successes were tempered by the imposition of weight penalties. By the middle of 1996, A4s were carrying an extra 95kg (218lb) more than a front-wheel drive car with a 30kg (68lb) penalty. Many people saw this as a swingeing punishment for its clear traction advantage, while others were of the opinion that weight penalties should be given on a handicapping basis to the most successful drivers.

Audi are no strangers to weight penalties, having had them imposed in TransAm racing. The ballast factor was reduced by 30kg (68lb) at mid-season in 1997 and the performance of both A4s improved dramatically. However, since 4WD is to be banned for 1998, Audi will have to think again.

The Audi pits crew cheers number two driver John Bintcliffe at Donington, where he finished a creditable sixth and fourth in the opening rounds in the team's second A4.

BMW Team Schnitzer

With a racing pedigree going back to the early 1960s, Schnitzer-BMW has always been a winning team, and the 320i models often fulfilled their promise in 1996, finishing runners-up in the Team and Manufacturers' categories.

Since the mid-1960s BMW has grown dramatically as a powerful force in top-class motor racing, and several private teams have represented the Munich firm in different areas of the sport. One such is the Bavarian Schnitzer team, which originated back in 1963. Its early successes included the German Touring Car Championship in 1966 with the BMW 2000TI and the European hill-climb championship in 1968, 1969 and 1971 with the 2002TI, 2002tii and 2.8 Coupé.

There was success in single seaters too, with several front runners using Schnitzer-built BMW engines in the 1975 European F2 series. The title was won convincingly by Jacques Lafitte in a Martini-Schnitzer BMW. The main thrust of Herbert Schnitzer's operations was in touring cars, however. The team won the 1978 German national championship with a BMW 320, and Austrian veteran Dieter Quester took the European Touring Car honours in 1983 with a Schnitzer 635 CSL. In the late 1970s, Jo Winkelhock's late elder brother Manfred was a member of the BMW junior squad, along with Eddie Cheever and Marc Surer, which dominated German saloon car racing with 320is.

The mid-1980s was another halcyon period for the Schnitzer team, with Roberto Ravaglia and Gerhard

Berger contesting the European series. There were wins in the Spa-Francorchamps 24-Hours in 1985 and 1986, with Ravaglia in the Schnitzer team BMW 635CSi winning the title in 1986. It was the last significant success for the big coupé, which had come to prominence in 1981 when it took the European Touring Car Championship in the hands of Helmut Kelleners and Umberto Grano.

Waiting in the wings was the compact 3-Series M3. Roberto Ravaglia took the unique World Touring Car title for Schnitzer in 1987 in an M3, and it was the start of a long reign for this model as a winner in its class and often of the race itself.

A Roadworthy Racer

The M3 was a homologation special, sufficiently numerous to qualify as both road car and racing machine. But whereas this breed is notoriously temperamental in a road-going context, the M3 was relatively civilized. As a road car it was a superlative performer, and its reliability in endurance events like the Spa-Francorchamps and Nürburgring 24-Hours was phenomenal. M3s won the Spa classic in 1987, 1989, 1990, and 1992, and Venezuelan ace Johnny Cecotto still holds the touring-car lap record for Nürburgring's daunting old Nordschleife circuit. It worked as a BTCC winner too, with Will Hoy taking the title in an M3 in 1991. The M3 was sturdy, and it proved itself as a rally car when Bernard Beguin won the 1987 Tour of Corsica.

The M3's successor, the new-shape 318i coupé was raced in

Tim Harvey took the 1992 title in a Vic Lee Motorsport-prepared BMW 318is Coupé; the BMW's ballast penalty was reduced for the second half of the season.

the BTCC in 1992. In its four-door format, Jo Winkelhock and Steve Soper were first and second in Schnitzer 318is in 1993. Jo won the Asia Pacific series in 1994, and, taking a sabbatical from the BTCC, he whisked away the German D1 ADAC Super Touring crown from under Frank Biela's nose in 1995, driving a Schnitzer 320i. Meanwhile Steve Soper won the Japanese series for Schnitzer, while Winkelhock and Peter Kox won the 1995 Spa-Francorchamps 24-Hours.

McLaren's Input

The 1996 version of the Uli Schiefer-designed 320i had the benefit of input from McLaren Cars in Woking (a benefit accruing from the BMW-engined McLaren F1 GT car) and was linked with BMW GB in a technical development programme, with engines built by Paul Rosche's facility at BMW's Munich headquarters.

After a year away, the Schnitzer team returned to the BTCC with Roberto Ravaglia partnering Jo Winkelhock. Before the season got under way, it had been thought that hard-charging Dutchman Peter Kox, who finished second to Winkelhock in the German Super Touring series in 1995, would be part of the BTCC assault. Eventually Kox was assigned to McLaren to test F1 cars and the analytical Ravaglia got the BTCC job. Kox put in some sterling drives in the BTCC towards the end of the season, helping BMW gain the Team prize for the Schnitzer team at selected rounds late in the year.

Some were surprised to find the Schnitzer BMWs winning so soon in 1996. Smokin' Jo won four times in the first half of the season, while Ravaglia's first BTCC win came at Silverstone. The purist still believes that rear drive is the only configuration for a racing car but BMW is saddled with a weight penalty for this advantage.

Jubilation on the Silverstone pit wall in 1993 as the Schnitzer team salutes Jo Winkelhock in the 318s. He was the first non-Briton to capture the BTCC title since 1973. Winkelhock and team-mate Soper were highly successful in 1993.

Ford Team Mondeo

Ford has always been a key player on the Touring Car stage, and when its Mondeo V6 entered the fray in 1993, it looked as if Ford was back in business; but Paul Radisich struggled vainly to match his early success.

After a lean year in 1995, Ford Motorsport switched its BTCC programme from Andy Rouse's RouseSport to Dick Bennetts' West Surrey Racing Team. For Ford, this was a fairly obvious choice, given New Zealander Bennetts' meticulous attention to detail, and his record of bringing on new talent and winning races. His team has won five British F3 titles and launched the careers of no less than 10 Grand Prix stars including Ayrton Senna, Mika Hakkinen, Rubens Barrichello and Jonathan Palmer.

Bennetts set up the team in 1980, having twice guided Keke Rosberg to the Formula Pacific Championship crown, and masterminded Niki Lauda's success in the 1979 BMW Procar Championship. He went on to engineer the F3 cars for Ron Dennis' winning Project Four team.

Jonathan Palmer was West Surrey Racing's first star,

winning the British Formula 3 series in 1981. It was Ayrton Senna's turn in 1983; the brilliant Brazilian won the first nine races of the season, a feat which no-one has bettered. Others who followed include Eddie Irvine and West Surrey Racing's 70th race win was notched up by Cristiano da Matta at Oulton Park in 1995.

A Glorious Heritage

West Surrey Racing's move into touring cars can also be seen as another reflection of the status of the BTCC. In running the works Mondeos, the team joins a long and exalted heritage of successes. Since 1957, Ford has been the manufacturer with most victories in the British Touring Car Championship. They have 206 wins to date – 152 more than the nearest rival Chevrolet. The Sierra Cosworth RS500 won 40 consecutive races between September 1987 and October 1990, making it the model with the longest unbroken string of successes.

But the most remarkable achievement goes back to a run of successes unmatched before or since, between

An ignominious exit for the Ford team at Donington's 1996 round one: both cars visited the gravel trap when Robertson spun on lap five.

May 1963 and June 1969. Every British touring car round was won outright by a Ford of one sort or another – Galaxie, Falcon, Mustang, Lotus-Cortina, Anglia and Escort.

A high-speed trio: Radisich's Mondeo leads Ravaglia's BMW and Cleland's Vectra along Top Straight before setting up for Paddock Bend at Brands Hatch in April 1996.

Electronic Wizardry

The four-door version of the Mondeo Si, with its Cosworth-built V6 engine, debuted midway through the 1993 BTCC calendar, and was the late-season pace-setter. Like all top BTCC runners, it carried on-board data-logging equipment, in this case the £12,000 Stack ST800 system, linked by sensors to a black box in the engine bay. With Team Leader Andy Rouse usually playing a supporting role, New Zealander Paul Radisich won three times in the RouseSport-prepared cars, and ended the season third in the drivers' points tally.

The following year was rather bleaker, with the Mondeo Ghias unable to match the winged Alfas, despite some good placings. This was such a sore point that the Team protested about the Alfas' aerodynamic aids – in vain as it turned out, leading Rouse to criticize the trend towards 'homologation specials'. Pretty soon everyone had sprouted the same wings. But Radisich scored two wins at Silverstone and Donington, and came back with a vengeance to win the end of season FIA Touring Car World Cup and the celebrated 20-lap TOCA Shootout, both at Donington. Radisich earned the £12,000 first prize for his victory in the second event.

For 1995, Radisich was teamed with Kelvin Burt in the Mondeo Ghias and finished the season in sixth place in the points standings. Privateer Matt Neal won the Privateers' Total Cup in a Mondeo, coming 21st overall, and another Mondeo runner, Aussie privateer Charlie Cox, finished 1995 in 22nd spot, having placed fifth at Brands in round three.

The 1996 five-door Mondeo featured a revised front subframe layout, which enabled the V6 engine to be shifted further back and canted over on its side in a bid to improve weight distribution. Unfortunately the resulting oil pick-up problems caused an ongoing headache for the team and a dearth of decent results.

West Surrey Racing received extra technical support from Schubel Engineering in Germany and single-seater specialists Reynard Racing Cars in Bicester. In addition to Paul Radisich, Team Mondeo had the services of former champ Will Hoy in 1997. The 1997 Mondeos were designed and built by John Piper at Reynard Racing Cars' Special Vehicle Projects operation. Their Ford Probe-based V6 engines were completely reworked by Jon Hilton at Cosworth Engineering. There is no doubt that Ford will be back on the pace sooner or later.

Team Honda Sport

The rigours of a steep learning curve bore fruit with David Leslie's success at the 1996 British GP curtain-raiser, and with James Thompson and Gabriele Tarquini at the helm the Accords were frontrunners in 1997.

Honda came to prominence in motor racing with its forays into Formula 1 with Richie Ginther in 1965 and John Surtees in 1967, subsequently winning numerous titles on two and four wheels. The company was, of course, the motive power behind six consecutive F1 World Constructors' Championships for the Williams and McLaren teams between 1986 and 1991. On a rather more mundane level, successes in Britain include the 1994 RAC National Junior Rally title, and the National Saloon Car Cup for standard production cars in 1993 and 1994, with the class-winning Group N 1600cc Honda Civic.

Then in 1995, Honda jumped in at the deep end of touring car racing with its Swindon-built Accord 2.0i LSs, entering them in the German, Belgian and British Super

James Kaye didn't have a good time at Oulton Park in 1996, his Accord finishing round nine in 13th place and ending round 10 with an accident.

Touring Championships. They managed to achieve some remarkable results, given the steep learning curve that they had to scale.

A Gradual Ascent
Their drivers were the experienced Scotsman David Leslie, a single-seater and World Sportscar Championship expert who had driven an Ecurie Ecosse Cavalier to good effect in previous BTCCs, and saloon car racer James Kaye from Harrogate. Leslie was also retained as Honda Motor Europe's test and development driver. There were some high finishes, sometimes running in close company, and their debut season saw Leslie finish eighth in the BTCC, with a best result of third in round 23 at Oulton Park. Kaye's best finish was a fifth at Knockhill, and towards the end of the season it was evident that the cars were coming good.

At the beginning of the 1996 season the Accords were running in the lower reaches of the top 10, but by

round seven at Silverstone, David Leslie had a third place finish and further top five placings looked feasible later in the year. Meanwhile James Kaye was dogged by a spate of bad luck, including something as elementary as a flat battery and the Brands Hatch decibel noise-meter, which meant he started from the back of the grid in rounds 13 and 14. The most astonishing thing happened at Silverstone for the Grand Prix support races – rounds 15 and 16 – when David Leslie put the Accord, with its new 320bhp engine, on pole position for both races. Nudged aside by Ravaglia in the first race, Leslie gave the Honda its much-deserved maiden victory in the second one. His success prompted a rush of rumours which incorrectly identified John Cleland and Derek Warwick as candidates for Honda drives in 1997.

Honda UK's managing director Toshio Ishino described their involvement in the BTCC as 'Very encouraging; the Accord adapted itself very well to the specific demands of close-fought motor racing.' While Mr Ishino's aspirations for a Championship-winning season may be some way off yet, there is no doubt now that Honda has the potential to be a championship winner, and once it commits itself there is every chance it'll persevere until success is achieved.

Solid Back-up

The team chosen to run the cars was the Milton Keynes-based firm Motor Sport Developments, which has a long and successful history in rallying. Formed some 20 years ago, the team operated as a subsidiary of General Motors as GM Eurosport with veteran rallyist and now Safety Devices roll-cage supremo Tony Fall at the helm. They ran the works Opel rally cars from their British base. When the team became independent in 1990, it took the name Motor Sport Developments and continued exclusively to develop Astras, Corsas and Calibras for General Motors. GM was promoting models like the Astra in smaller markets so Astras were prepared by MSD to contest the Portuguese Touring Car Championship and the SATCAR series in South Africa. They were the winning cars in both the Portuguese and South African series in 1993, and second in 1994 with seven victories in Portugal and eight in South Africa, where Mike Briggs was second in the Championship.

From mid-season in 1996 the Honda Accord began to fulfil its promise in the hands of David Leslie, with a fabulous win at the Silverstone Grand Prix meeting. Leslie's MSD-run Honda is pictured at Brands Hatch in April.

Having established a foothold in circuit racing, MSD made a concerted effort to link up with a car manufacturer, and Honda was first choice. The bodyshells came from Honda's Swindon plant, and the engines were built by noted Mugen-Honda specialist Neil Brown.

It all finally came good for Team MSD when Leslie triumphed in the Grand Prix support race at Silverstone, a feat that confirmed the Accord's potential in the final rounds of 1996. The team came fifth in Manufacturer and Team categories.

It was all change during the winter lay-off; Honda said goodbye to MSD and went over to former BMW and Alfa Romeo experts Prodrive, while MSD were welcomed aboard by Peugeot. Race preparation of the Accords was in the hands of Prodrive's chief engineer Keith Knott, formerly a race engineer at Ray Mallock's Vauxhall operation, as well as project leader on Lola Cars' Indycar programme. Like the Audi A4, the Accords benefit from a double wishbone suspension set-up all round. Their engines continued to be built by Neil Brown, with support from Honda's own R and D division in Japan. There were new drivers at Honda too, in the shape of James Thompson from Vauxhall and 1994 BTCC Champion Gabriele Tarquini. By mid season, the Italian was fourth in the hunt for the title.

Esso Ultron Team Peugeot

The 406 might be one of the neatest-looking Super Touring cars, but during 1996 and 1997 BTCC Harvey and Watts grappled with minor mishaps with little reward. Things could only get better.

Like Renault, Peugeot's motor racing heritage is as old as the motor car itself, having won the 1894 Paris-Rouen trials. A venerable precedent indeed. Like Alfa and Mercedes Benz, Peugeot was a competitor in early Grands Prix as well as the 1913 Indianapolis 500. But its more recent background has been in rallying rather than circuit racing. Peugeots have always been noted for their robust design, and in 1968 a 505 won the London-Sydney Marathon. Coming more up-to-date, Peugeots were victorious in the World Rally Championship in 1981, 1985 and 1986.

While Patrick Watts won the British Esso Group N Saloon Car title for Peugeot in 1991, the company's resources were assigned to conquering the World

For 1996, Patrick Watts moved on from a 405 to the new 406 – seen here at Oulton Park in August, where a first-lap accident put him out of both races.

Sportscar Championship. It succeeded in its first season, the Peugeot 905 winning all but one round. The following year Peugeot 905s scored a memorable 1-2-3 at the Le Mans 24-Hours, and in 1994 Peugeot turned its attentions to Formula 1, supplying first McLaren and currently Jordan with F1 engines.

A Difficult Switch

In 1992 Peugeot was tempted into the BTCC arena by TOCA, but driver Robb Gravett and Peugeot's rally-orientated engineers had little luck sorting out the 405Mi16 in 1992 and 1993. Having moved from Mazda to Peugeot for 1994, Patrick Watts made a typically doughty showing in the 405Mi16, finishing eighth in the Championship, but his team-mate Eugene O'Brien did not have such a good time of it.

Watts slipped to 10th in the 1995 points tally, although he scored a second place at Snetterton and a

third at Thruxton. Simon Harrison was regularly a finisher in the 1995 season, albeit a lowly 24th in the points. Privateer Hamish Irvine also contested the Total Cup with a 405, coming fourth in that category, but, more often than not, last in the races.

For its fifth season in the BTCC, Peugeot entered the all-new, French-developed 406 Super Tourer. The new model had a longer wheelbase and wider track, as well as a stiffer shell than its predecessor, an inherently more stable layout. This was a tribute not only to the new design but also to the roll cage construction. Its stiffness meant that suspension settings could be more accurate.

The 406 racer, engineered by Steve Ridgers, had better weight distribution than the old model. There were five-way adjustable dampers at the front, and at the rear a new multi-link suspension system compensated for roll. Suspension components were lighter and the set-up was stiffer, and it was a better aerodynamic package in terms of downforce and drag elimination; the greater front overhang allowed for a more effective front splitter and undertray than had been possible with the 405.

Drivers for 1996 were Watts and 1992 BTCC Champion Tim Harvey. They were closely matched at several rounds, although a series of minor mechanical failures and accidents marred the first few rounds.

Although the 406 was successful in the German Super Touring series, Watts and team-mate Tim Harvey had a frustrating season in the BTCC; a stiffer front end indicated promise for 1997.

Motor Sport Developments' managing director David Whitehead led a technical team which included Mike Pilbeam, famous for designing the Motul-sponsored BRM P201 Formula 1 car driven by Pescarolo and Beltoise in 1974. Pilbeam's other claim to fame is the construction of the single-seater Pilbeam hillclimb cars, which have won the British Hillclimb Championship several years running.

Based at Bourne, Lincolnshire, Pilbeam's role was to initiate the engineering for the 406's suspension and chassis set-up. The engines were prepared by former Mini-dicer extraordinaire and 1978 BTCC champion Richard Longman. Other key MSD personnel included team manager Paul Risbridger, a former member of the Peugeot BTCC squad, while race engineer Eddie Hinckley was formerly with Tom Walkinshaw at TWR. Adrian Scott was marketing chief, and Graham Garvin was second race engineer. Results gained in the first half of 1997 were little better than the previous year's, however, and Peugeot's points tally was down at the bottom end of the chart, only slightly up on Ford's.

Vodaphone Nissan Racing

Backed by Nissan Motorsports Europe, the RML team at Wellingborough succeeded in turning the midfield-running Primera into a BTCC front-runner in 1997.

Gary Ayles' Primera at Knockhill during the fruitless 1996 season. The team missed several rounds while getting the Nissan engine and chassis sorted.

Despite Andy Rouse's long legacy of touring car successes and a promising start with the Mondeos in 1993, his three years spent running Ford's official BTCC team brought the Dagenham manufacturer no lasting success. So they parted company, and for 1996 RouseSport was engaged by Nissan Motorsports Europe to turn the Primera into a regular race winner.

It didn't happen, and for 1997, Nissan's representative in the BTCC was Ray Mallock Ltd. Fresh from three season's Vectra- and Cavalier-fettling, RML was well placed to turn the 1997-spec Primera GT into a potential front runner. The project was handled by Graham Humphries, one-time Spice Group C and Lola Cars engineer, at RML's modern Wellingborough race headquarters. As the old adage goes, a new broom

sweeps clean, and the Primera's old Hewland six-speed gearbox was promptly switched for a six-speed sequential Xtrac model, while John Judd's Rugby-based Engine Developments firm got the engine preparation contract instead of RouseSport. A celebrated engine specialist, Judd built the Formula 1 Yamaha V10 engines for TWR-Arrows in 1997.

Legacy of Success

RML team principal Ray Mallock is the son of Arthur Mallock, who designed and built the ubiquitous U2 Clubmans Formula sportscars. Ray was no mean racer himself in the 1970s and '80s. Involved with the Ecurie Ecosse World Sportscar Championship programme in the mid-1980s for wealthy patron Hugh McCaig, Ray also engineered the Nimrod Aston Martin project for Le Mans. Budgets were astronomical, and the scheme foundered. Touring cars were a more economical proposition, and Mallock prepared a pair of ex-works

Cavaliers for the 1992 season for David Leslie and Harry Nuttall, running under the Ecurie Ecosse banner. By 1995 Mallock was building Cavalier Touring Cars for customers world-wide as well as the works' BTCC cars, and in 1996 RML built the bodies as well. When Nissan beckoned at the end of 1996, RML began a new chapter.

Although no newcomers to the Supertouring scene – the Primera eGT had seen plenty of action in the German, Italian and Spanish championships during 1995 – 1996 had been very much a learning year for Nissan and RouseSport.

Drivers for the 1996 BTCC were tin-top specialist Gary Ayles, who had already driven for Rouse in Toyotas, and Formula 3 cup-holder Owen McAuley. One of the most unlikely dramas happened to Gary Ayles at Brands Hatch when a hot exhaust ignited his seat belt harness, forcing him to retire from round 13 with a cockpit fire. All was quickly rectified, and he came 10th in the next race.

The team gambled on Yokohama tyres, which might have paid off in dry races, but when RouseSport ran Michelins in the wet at Oulton Park early in the year it was decided to make a switch. The Primeras ran on Michelin Pilots from round 13, and this meant Dunlop and Michelin were the only tyre manufacturers left in the BTCC. Gary Ayles debuted the new car at rounds 11 and 12 at Snetterton, but the cars were languishing somewhat in 10th and 14th places. The demanding time schedule of the BTCC makes it difficult to evaluate a new car before its launch, but this was not a bad demonstration; it is estimated that the honing of a Super Touring car can take three seasons before it is ready to become a regular winner. Meanwhile McAuley was not best pleased at being saddled with the unreliable 1995 car and quit halfway through the season.

A change of driver line-up as well as team management for 1997 saw Scot Anthony Reid partner David Leslie in the Primera squad. It was also a time for reunions of a sort. Leslie was now back in the RML fold, having raced the Ecurie Ecosse Cavaliers successfully back in 1993, while Reid was no newcomer to Nissan, having driven a RouseSport prepared Primera for the Italian BMS team in the German Supertourenwagen series in 1996. Both RML drivers brought their extensive experience and race-craft into play, and with the mechanical innovations, there was no question that the Primeras were now capable of being on-the-pace. Although sometimes in the wars and at the heart of controversial moves – in Reid's case in particular – they were very often in contention during the first half-season of 1997.

A lowly 13th at Brands Hatch in the previous year's Primera, Owen McAuley was so disenchanted with its performance that he quit the team midway through 1996.

TOM'S Toyota

Although strictly a private team, Lee Brookes' 1996 operation had support from TOM'S GB and thus a direct link with Toyota itself. Brookes achieved his ambition to lift the privateers' Total Cup.

Team Brookes, 1996 debutantes, were a new privateer outfit. The team was created by Brookes Motorsport to run a 1995 Toyota Carina for Renault Clio Cup champion Lee Brookes to contest the Total Cup. The team received technical support from Hingham, Norfolk-based TOM'S Toyota.

TOM'S has been involved with Toyota's racing programmes in World Sportscars and Formula 3 as well as the BTCC, and built the Team Brookes car in 1995 for Julian Bailey. However, the team's progress was hampered during the 1996 BTCC because of power understeer – where the car refuses to turn into a bend unless the driver comes off the accelerator.

Boss of TOM'S GB is Hiroshi Fushida, 50, who was the first Japanese driver to attempt to qualify for a Grand

Prix – at Zandvoort in 1975 with the Maki-Ford – and whose racing career also includes stints in CanAm with a McLaren M12 and UOP Shadow, and TransAm, which resulted in a couple of broken legs. He drove at Le Mans three times before dropping out in 1981 to manage his family's kimono busness.

An Inspirational Leader

Mr Fushida re-emerged in 1986 to run the Dome sports-racing team – including ex-Volvo driver Jan Lammers – to maintain the factory's racing programme. As well as the BTCC Carinas, Mr Fushida co-ordinates TOM'S effort in the British Formula 3 series, which in 1996 ran Toyota-powered Dallara 036Fs. A Le Mans-type sports-racing prototype is the most recent project at TOM'S GB.

In 1992, the TOM'S-run Toyota Carinas were campaigned by reigning BTCC Champion Will Hoy, partnered by Andy Rouse. The new BTCC regulations provided Rouse with a challenge to develop the Toyota

Julian Bailey heads for fourth place at the 1995 Silverstone GP meeting, a season which saw his Carina E regularly in the top eight.

Carina into a racing car, and it was quickly on the pace, although lacking the consistency of the BMWs. Will came second in the BTCC, winning two races, while Rouse won the final round at Silverstone.

Toyota's next ace was erstwhile F-1 driver Julian Bailey. He transferred to the TOM'S Toyota team in 1991 and spent the following four seasons with the Carina. His best season was 1993, which he ended in fifth place. For the TOM'S team it was a downward slide in the BTCC, with Bailey achieving 12th place overall in 1994, although there was a slight improvement in 1995, Julian finishing ninth in the points table.

Meanwhile, the Carina's fortunes dwindled to the extent that for 1996 they were in the hands of what

was ostensibly an independent outfit. Like all privateers, Lee Brookes used one of the previous season's cars, with its origins in the Norfolk workshops of TOM'S GB and the Cologne-based Toyota Team Europe. For a while it looked as though the dramatic progress of Richard Kaye in the Mint Motorsport Cavalier might upset Brookes' bid for the privateers' title. For 1997, Brookes defended his title with an ex-works Peugeot 406, and the competition was even fiercer.

Throughout 1996, Lee Brookes was the man to beat in terms of consistency for Total Cup honours, although his Carina generally finished in the lower orders of the actual BTCC.

Williams Renault

As the BTCC goes from strength to strength, the big names of motor sport are drawn to it, and since 1995 the yellow and blue Lagunas have been run by Frank Williams' mighty Didcot-based F1 operation.

Perhaps the most ringing endorsement of the BTCC's status as a motor sport 'superpower' was the decision of the multiple world championship-winning Williams F1 team to join the fray in 1995, taking over the running of the factory-backed Renault team. 'It is appropriate that Williams be involved in the BTCC,' Frank Williams said. 'Next to F1, the BTCC is the most important series in the world outside America.'

Williams' presence, and its subsequent success in the 1995 Manufacturers' Championship, upped the ante among the top teams, moving them on to a higher level of technical and commercial sophistication. Renault UK managing director Michel Gigou justified the company's

Time for a quick change of tyres in the pits garage for Alain Menu as a rain shower interrupts proceedings at Oulton Park.

involvement thus, 'Motor sport adds a dynamic edge to the flair which distinguishes Renault from other makes, and we know for sure that the impact of our participation and success in the BTCC is excellent. It reinforces the importance of creating this dynamic image. Every race we win adds value to our success.' Renault ran a series of creative outdoor posters and adverts featuring the Laguna's BTCC race wins and, ultimately, the 1995 manufacturers' title.

A Difficult Start

Renault UK has had a presence in the BTCC since 1993 when it ran the R19 for Alain Menu and Tim Harvey, but although both won races it was generally considered a car that should have been shot at birth. The highlight of 1993 was a one-two success at Donington at the Easter European Grand Prix meeting when it teemed down

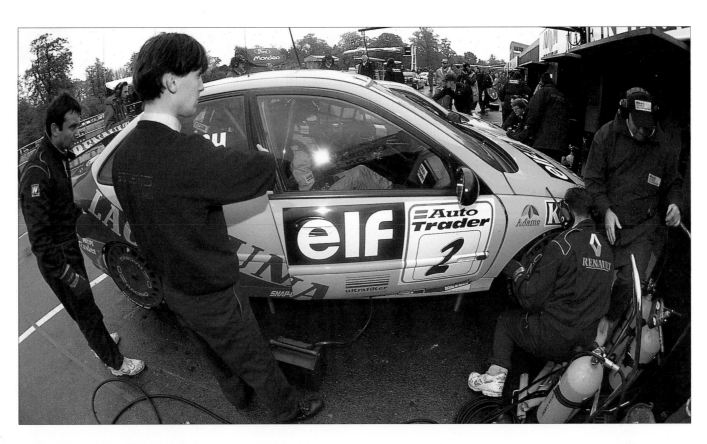

with rain. For drivers and team, it was a learning year, assessing suspension set-ups and sorting the sequential gearbox, all vital groundwork.

The new Laguna appeared in 1994, again with Menu and Harvey at the helm. The cars proved to be fast but fragile, and while it was Menu who grabbed the headlines, Harvey proved to be more of a workhorse. Renault came second overall in the BTCC with two wins and three second places.

Reaching for the Top

The Laguna proved the quickest car in the late stages of the 1995 season, Alain Menu claiming runner-up spot in the Drivers' championship for the second year running. With a total of 10 race victories by Menu and Will Hoy, and three one-two finishes, Renault was top of the Manufacturers' table. The cars run in the 1996 BTCC with the same driver line-up were entirely Williams-built, under the direction of Ian Harrison and a staff of 40 at Williams' Didcot base. They were immediately on the pace, challenging the four-wheel-drive Audis and the Volvo 850s, and regularly achieving top five placings. Menu's domination of the two Brands Hatch rounds at the end of June underlined the Laguna's excellence on fast, curving circuits, and the ups and downs of Brands presents a special challenge.

Ravaglia's BMW is the meat in a Renault sandwich. Menu, leading here, was generally quicker and more fortunate than 1996 Laguna team-mate Hoy.

Menu pipped Rydell for second place in the 1996 Drivers' Championship, with Will Hoy ninth, while Renault were fourth in the Manufacturers' category, and in third place in the Team section. There was no question about it: Alain Menu was the man to catch during the first half of 1997, consistently on the podium and favourite for the champion's crown. Team-mate Jason Plato was never far behind, establishing the Laguna as class of the field.

The Lagunas' 16-valve iron-block, alloy head engines – which are worth a cool £40,000 each – are supplied by Magny-Cours-based specialists Moteurs Sodemo, who cater for Renault's racing and rally interests. Chief engineer is John Russell and team manager is Didier Debae. The Lagunas use Hewland's quick-change six-speed sequential gearbox – some £18,000-worth of kit. Braking power is provided by massive vented drilled discs and water-cooled AP six-piston calipers at the front and four-piston at the rear. The carbon-metallic pads and discs can reach 500°C (932°F) in the heat of battle yet are still capable of halting the car with dramatic speed.

Vauxhall Sport

Consistently the mainstay of the BTCC, the Vauxhall Cavalier was pensioned off in 1996 when the Vectra took over. But not before John Cleland had sewn up the 1995 Championship with the old warhorse.

From the model's introduction in 1990, Vauxhall Cavaliers were consistently the mainstay of the BTCC, run by the works Vauxhall Sport team and in 1992 and 1993 by Ecurie Ecosse. The works cars were built by Dave Cook Racing until 1994, when Vauxhall Sport switched to Ray Mallock's operation which had built and run the Ecurie Ecosse cars. The 1996 season was something of a debacle for Vauxhall, and in a pan-European rationalization of its competition activities, the BTCC programme was handed over to the Greatworth, Oxfordshire-based, Triple Eight racing team. The 1997 Vectras were now fettled under the guidance of former TWR Volvo chief designer John Gentry, while engines continued to be built by John Dunn's Swindon Engines.

A 1996 Vectra is fabricated in Ray Mallock's workshops at Wellingborough, Northants. Some 34 Mallock-built Vauxhalls compete in Super Touring racing all around the world.

The arrangement works well. Vauxhall Sport, under Mike Nicholson and competitions manager John Nixey, field the Super Touring cars as well as Formula Vauxhall and the company's rallying programme. They also provided the engines for Oliver Gavin's British Formula 3 Championship success in 1995. The chain of command goes via Walter Treser at Opel HQ in Russelsheim all the way to General Motors in Detroit. At a grass-roots level, the people who make it happen are those at Triple Eight.

Long-term Involvement

Ray Mallock's RML firm became involved in 1993 when, with more support from Vauxhall, Leslie took three pole positions and a victory at Thruxton. RML tendered for the works' contract and built four cars for the BTCC and another for a Japanese customer. Still alongside Jeff Allam at Vauxhall Sport, John Cleland scored two race wins in 1994 and took the BTCC title in 1995 with six wins. Taking into account points earned by James Thompson

and Mike Briggs in Cavaliers, Vauxhall took the BTCC Team prize, but were pipped for Manufacturers' crown by Renault. That year, RML built 10 Cavaliers for the BTCC and overseas customers, all right-hand drive, and 17 cars for 1996, which for marketing reasons are left-hand drive.

After the Cavalier's championship success for John Cleland, Vauxhall moved on to the Vectra for 1996. RML was in charge of the Vauxhall Sport programme for the third year running, and there was a great deal of testing at Jarama and Jerez circuits in Spain, at Vallelunga in Italy, and at nearly all the British circuits. The Vectra had good turn-in qualities but more oversteer in high-speed corners than desirable. It was powered by the 16-valve twin-cam unit, developed by Swindon Racing Engines to give 295bhp at 8,400rpm. The Mallock-developed suspension system included McPherson struts with lightweight lower wishbones and rocker-activated steel anti-roll bar at the front. It also had twin lateral links coupled to an aerospace-spec steel trailing arm, plus coaxial spring damper units mounted to the trailing arms at the rear. It produced a stiffness some five times firmer than a road-going set-up.

Firm Guidance
In 1996 the team continued to be well in contention with patriarch John Cleland sometimes having to speak

sternly to his thrusting young partner James Thompson. Until Thompson's Snetterton victory, the Vectras tended to be just inside or just outside the top five: well in contention but not quite able to see off the Audis, Volvos, BMWs and Renaults. A revised steering system was introduced in July 1996, which both drivers considered an improvement.

Mallock built two new Vectras in mid-1996, vindicated by Thompson's Snetterton triumph. The bodyshells, previously prepared by Matter in Germany, were now fettled in-house by Mallock. This arrangement was transferred to Triple Eight, who would produce new cars by halfway through the 1997 season.

Meanwhile, John Cleland was joined in the Vectra squad for 1997 by former F1 star and erstwhile Alfa Romeo 155 driver Derek Warwick, and it looked as if such a formidable pairing might carry all before it. During the early part of the season, the Scot generally found himself out-qualified by the Jerseyman. However the Vectras lacked grip in the early part of the season, although by mid-term they were getting on terms with the race leaders.

An impressive John Cleland two-wheels his way to second and first places in rounds 11 and 12 at Brands Hatch, en route to the 1995 BTCC title.

TWR-Volvo

Publicity from the 850 Estate and the high-scoring 850 Saloon enhanced Volvo's image tremendously, while the more conventional S40 continued to strengthen TWR's reputation in 1997.

Tom Walkinshaw Racing, Volvo's BTCC partner, has always been in motor sport to win, and founder Tom Walkinshaw has vast personal experience, from Formula Atlantic and Capris to Jaguars and Rover Vitesses. Apart from European Touring Car success with the XJ-S in 1984, TWR Jaguar XJRs were World Sportscar champions in 1987, 1988 and 1991, and they won twice at Le Mans and at the Daytona 24-Hours.

More recently, Tom Walkinshaw has been deeply involved with F1, masterminding Benetton's World Championship victories in 1994 and 1995, as well as holding technical control of Ligier in 1995. TWR acquired a major stake in the Arrows F1 team in 1996, although there was a conspicuous lack of success for Damon Hill during 1997.

Apart from its prowess on the track, TWR built the XJ220 Jaguar supercars at its Bloxham factory from 1992, and designed and engineered the Aston Martin DB7 – one of the finest looking cars of all time – in 1993. An arrangement with Volvo in 1995 saw TWR producing coupé and cabriolet models based on the 850 from a purpose-built plant at Uddevalla in Sweden.

The TWR pit crew are jubilant as Rickard Rydell's Volvo 850 takes the chequered flag to win at Knockhill in 1996, his second win of the season.

There was also a deal with GM in Australia to create niche-model Holdens. TWR ran General Motors' Holden Commodore V8s in events like the Bathurst 1000.

The company struck a deal with Volvo in 1993 to run the 850s in the BTCC, and, after careful consideration, elected to use the estate model. It was a marvellous publicity coup, banishing Volvo's traditional association with the rather stuffy antique dealers and gymkhana set. A learning season followed in 1994, with Jan Lammers and Rickard Rydell generally mid-field runners in the five-cylinder 850 Estates; the cars were fast on the straights but not hugely impressive in cornering.

Serious Challengers

In 1995 the TWR Volvo 850 saloons of Tim Harvey and Rydell did much better, with Rickard winning at Donington, Silverstone, Oulton and Knockhill, and achieving several high placings for third place in the BTCC points table. Harvey was a creditable fifth, with two wins at Brands Hatch. The Volvos were third in the Manufacturers' league, behind Renault and Vauxhall.

Up to mid-season in 1996 there was a win apiece for Rydell and Kelvin Burt at Oulton Park and Silverstone respectively, and there was high praise for the build quality of the Volvo and its componentry after Kelvin suffered a dreadful accident at Oulton Park.

TWR has blossomed from a motor racing specialist into a sizeable automotive manufacturing and general engineering concern, operating from a 12 hectare (30 acre) base at Leafield, 32km (20 miles) west of Oxford.

TWR's Super Touring S40 Racing team is led by director Roger Sillman. The S40s are powered by 20-valve five-cylinder engines, producing 290bhp at 8500rpm, and their predecessors, the 850s, were the first cars in the BTCC to run with catalytic converters. Several of the Volvo's key components are specially manufactured items; the power-assisted rack-and-pinion steering and the front-suspension McPherson struts are TWR developments.

Volvo stands the best chance of raising its profile in the BTCC. 'It's the championship with the greatest

The BTCC drivers are an amiable lot, and Kelvin Burt takes time out to sign autographs on race programmes for the fans at Brands Hatch.

guests, new business prospects, dealers, car owners and incentive scheme prize-winners, from 26 different countries, were entertained at various BTCC events. Volvo itself makes the most of its BTCC participation and successes in its international marketing and advertising.

The S40s were built at TWR's Leafield facility under new chief designer Brendan Gribben. Their immediate advantage over the 850 was aerodynamic, being a narrower and more rounded design. Engines continued to be built in-house by TWR Race Engines, overseen by Charlie Bamber. During the first half of the 1997 season, Rydell put his S40 to rather better use than Burt, although the pair had a memorable scrap at Silverstone. The Swede was possibly the hardest charger on the track, and was the driver most likely to offer anything like a credible challenge to the Lagunas.

international reach, and Volvo's BTCC programme gives its regional marketing companies a platform on which to build on the company's new image,' said TWR/Volvo Racing's marketing manager Andy King. TWR's marketing arm services Volvo's regional markets worldwide, dishing out promotional literature and hosting TWR's trackside hospitality suite. All teams use similar promotional strategies to a certain extent, of course, but a measure of TWR's success in that field is that during the 1995 season, nearly 3000 Volvo VIPs, including corporate

Burt's Volvo 850 heads Will Hoy's Laguna, James Thompson's Vectra and Paul Radisich's Mondeo during BTCC 1996 round 14 at Brands Hatch.

Team Dynamics

Based around Matt Neal, Team Dynamics has been a BTCC contender since 1992, running BMW M3, Mazda Xedos and Mondeo. It has also been at the forefront of the Total Cup battle, which Matt won handsomely in 1995.

The team was originally established by Steve Neal and Ray Bellm to sustain Tim Harvey's bid for the 1992 BTCC crown with a BMW 318. In 1994 the team built a Mazda 323 to contest the Donington World Cup event, but abandoned it in favour of a Mondeo. Team Dynamics was re-formed in 1995 to give the 1993 privateers' champion Matt Neal (Steve's son) a further chance of Total Cup glory using the Rouse-built ex-Philippe Gache Ford Mondeo. The gambit paid off. Neal was the runaway winner of the lucrative Total prize, and even embarrassed the works Mondeos on more than one occasion. As Ford shifted teams from RouseSport to West Surrey Racing at the end of the 1995 season, Team Dynamics was also in the frame for the works contract.

Team principal is Steve Neal, who has two claims to fame. He is also boss of Rimstock Alloy Wheels, and back in the 1960s and early 1970s was a star driver in the British Vita-sponsored Mini Cooper S team. Neal partnered tyre-smoking wizard John Rhodes in contesting the 1300cc class in the British Saloon Car Championship, and later the Cooper-Britax-Downton team alongside Gordon Spice.

After a late start in 1996, Matt Neal finished as high as 11th at Thruxton – good going for a privateer – but it was altogether a patchy first half-season. The team's absence at certain rounds, coupled with minor component failures and an accident, left the Total Cup category under-subscribed, with Carina driver Lee Brookes and Richard Kaye's Cavalier in sole contention.

The main problem that afflicted the Team Dynamics Mondeo in 1997 was a voracious appetite for Michelin front tyres. But Matt Neal was back in contention again for Total Cup points, dominating the proceedings at mid-season.

Total Cup contender Matt Neal approaches Druids Hairpin at Brands Hatch in the Team Dynamics Mondeo on his way to 16th place in round four, 1996.

Mint Motorsport

In 1996 Richard Kaye was clearly the fastest of the Total Cup privateers, with far and away the greatest number of wins in that category. For 1997, the challenge was taken up by Jamie Wall.

Mint Motorsport was a new team created specially for privateer Richard Kaye's Championship debut in 1995. The team's owners, Brian Ellis and Paul Andrews, continued in 1996 with an ex-works Ray Mallock-prepared Vauxhall Cavalier in place of the Ford Mondeo campaigned the previous season. In pre-BTCC testing, Kaye was actually quicker than the new works Vectras.

Regarded as the season's 'flyer', Richard's attainments in 1996 included starting from 11th on the grid at Donington for round two, only 1.8 seconds down on pole, no mean achievement for an independent driver. He set the widest margin on the grid between Total Cup competitors – he was 4.726 seconds faster than Lee Brookes at Oulton Park's round nine. In round 10 he slipped on oil on the track between Cascades and Island bend and the FujiFilm Cavalier shot backwards into the barrier. Although apparently a total wreck, it was resuscitated by the Mint Motorsport mechanics and he bounced back from another big one at Knockhill.

Richard's father, Peter Kaye, was in charge of engineering and team management. Proof of his abilities was based on a peculiar accolade: the team had the distinction of completing the fastest engine change, in a scant two hours between races at Thruxton.

At mid-season 1996, only Jeff Allam had a better finishing record than Richard Kaye, out of all drivers who started 20 rounds of the BTCC since 1991. And in 1996, only Frank Biela stood on the podium more times than Richard – whose Total Cup wins allowed him up there. In 1997, the Mint Motorsport drive went to the ex-Ford XR2 and Rover 220 Turbo racer Jamie Wall, who put in some determined drives against Total Cup rivals.

Richard Kaye had a couple of monumental crashes in the ex-works Cavalier during 1996, but was often challenging the works cars – as he was here at Snetterton.

The Cars

They look like the everyday family saloons we drive on the road. But under the skin lies a sophisticated racing car, built to a specific set of rules to ensure competitive racing. Their track success reflects the way each car is set-up to accommodate these regulations.

Why are some cars quick on certain circuits yet apparently floundering on others? The answer lies in their specifications which, while complying with a strict set of regulations, are adapted by the teams' engineers to make their cars perform to their best advantage. And at some venues the topography of the track just doesn't suit them. Other factors include tyre characteristics, which may favour Dunlop at the expense of Michelin according to climate and surface, and vice-versa. Also, drivers have their own favourite circuits – Thruxton, for example, offers a very different set of challenges to those of Brands Hatch.

In this chapter we take the most important factory-based runners and identify the differences in each car's specification. While all are mass-produced four-door family saloons, they are actually highly sophisticated racing cars. The reason the factory runners are so closely matched is that their 2.0-litre engines are limited to 8500rpm, while modifications and tuning yield top speeds in excess of 255km/h (160mph). A seemingly perverse system of weight penalties equalizes the performance of front-wheel-drive, rear-wheel-drive, and four-wheel-drive cars. So while it may sometimes appear that the four-wheel-drive Audis are out of breath and lagging behind, they are in fact labouring under some 65kg (143lb) of ballast.

Specification

First requirement is a 2.0-litre engine, which almost every car manufacturer offers. An 8500rpm rev limit is activated by a Monk governor, ensuring power outputs don't vary widely, and from 1997 was monitored by TOCA using on-board data-logging equipment. Controversially, there is a system of weight limits designed to equalize the performance of front-, rear-, and four-wheel-drive cars.

A minimum length of 4.2 m (13ft 10in) means that it is mass-market family saloons which are used rather than smaller hot-hatches and super-minis. Their bodyshells must be identical to those of the road car from which they are derived, of which a minimum 25,000 must have been built.

However, the mechanical componentry, like engine and transmission, need only be based on a production run of 2500. From 1995, a revised set of rules allowed all cars to run with front spoilers and rear wings, which had more of an equalizing effect. The engines' maximum displacement of 2000cc can be achieved by means of boring out or sleeving down if necessary. The electronically controlled rev limit of 8500rpm is meant to aid reliability and limit development costs, but,

Action stations for Derek Warwick, as he dons his flame-retarding balaclava. He is also protected in the Alfa 155 cockpit by a hefty roll cage and window net.

Audi Sport mechanics prepare John Bintcliffe's A4 in the pits garage at Brands Hatch.

nevertheless, engine modifications and tuning mean that Super Touring cars are capable of top speeds in excess of 255km/h (160mph). At least 2500 examples of the production engine on which the race unit is based must have been built, but it can be borrowed from another model within the same manufacturer's model range. Engines with more than six cylinders are banned, as are turbocharging and supercharging. In order to prevent a spiral of escalating costs similar to those which swamped Formula 1 during the late 1980s and early 1990s, high-tech equipment such as traction control and active suspension is excluded from the BTCC.

The engine must remain on the same axis as in the road car – transverse or in-line – but for better balance and lower centre of gravity its location may be shifted a small way backwards or forwards and it may sit lower in

Qualifying consists of two 30-minute sessions. Here John Bintcliffe's Audi A4 gets its Dunlops swapped during practice at Knockhill.

the engine bay. Touring Cars are as green as possible in the 1990s, with unleaded fuel and catalytic converters being compulsory. As with motor sport in general these days, strict noise limits must also be adhered to. Too many decibels registering on the noise meter and the offending car gets sent to the back of the grid with a 10-second penalty.

Spare cars are not allowed, and drivers can only race the specific car that has been scrutineered for them at each meeting. Teams are allowed to change engines during a meeting so long as they get the scrutineers' approval. Also, an engine removed from a car must remain available for technical post-mortem.

While the majority of participants are front-wheel drive, the weight differentials between cars with front drive, rear drive and four-wheel drive are monitored carefully, and they may be adjusted by TOCA once during the year.

From 1996, the limits were 975kg (2155lb) for front-wheel drive, 1000kg (2210lb) for rear-wheel drive and

1070kg (2365lb) for four-wheel drive. A typical driver weight of 80kg (177lb) is added to these figures, meaning in effect that teams with lighter drivers must run more ballast in their cars. The weights of cars, with driver on board, are monitored several times over a race weekend, both during qualifying and in the regular scrutineering sessions.

Different Super Touring championships operate different parity controls. For instance, the Japanese rules have a weight penalty system in which ballast is added to the top three finishers in the first of a double-header meeting, and they then carry ballast for the second race.

In the BTCC, gearboxes must be mechanically operated and have a maximum of six forward speeds. In effect all cars have purpose-built six-speed, sequential shift boxes. Fully automatic gearboxes are not allowed. The car's suspension must be of the same type as that in the homologated road car, so there must be a McPherson strut in the same place as there is one on the road car – but purpose-built, fully-adjustable racing versions certainly are legitimately used.

Naturally, in-car safety is a vital factor and all bodyshells are fitted with massively strong tubular steel rollover cages. These also have the effect of virtually eliminating flexing of the body under cornering stresses, as well as ensuring the suspension mounting points are located rigidly, so suspension behaviour is not compromised.

Double fire extinguisher systems are plumbed-in, to automatically direct foam into the engine bay and cockpit. Racing seats are made of Kevlar, carbon fibre and steel and are very sturdy. Sitting low in the car, drivers are held firmly in place by six-point safety harnesses. A net is fitted in the window to place restriction on any movement of the head and arms in the event of an accident. From 1997, the door-bars were clad in composite panelling for greater driver protection.

Scrutineering
All race meetings nowadays involve their participants in scrutineering, which takes place before the day's racing starts. Competing BTCC cars may be subject to scrutineering checks at any time, but in practice all cars

Tyres are big business, allocation is strict, and choice can be crucial. The Lagunas' O.Z. wheels are shod with grooved slicks for dry races and treaded Michelins in case of rain.

are checked at the start of each meeting.

The chief scrutineer has the power to select cars to be checked after each qualifying session and after the race. If there is any hint of foul play, a team must submit the car concerned for further scrutiny for a period of 72 hours after a race. TOCA administrators can demand full access to all computers and team equipment for further analysis. These controls have the effect of maintaining fair play in the paddock.

Fuel
All BTCC cars run on standard unleaded fuel, provided by TOCA, who can make checks at any time during the

course of a meeting. Teams aren't allowed to refuel cars before the end of official practice or before completion of post-practice scrutineering.

Tyres

Each car is allowed six slick tyres per race. These have to be submitted for marking when the car is scrutineered. If more than two are damaged and unsafe, they can grant a maximum of two replacements, which must be

identical to the originals and approved by the scrutineers and the tyre companies. In addition, up to 16 'grooved' rain tyres may be used at each meeting, although each competitor is allowed one spare tyre during the championship season for use in case of genuine hardship. Tyre warmers and chemical treatments are strictly forbidden. The most prominent suppliers have been Michelin, Dunlop, and, up to 1995, Yokohama.

In 1996 and 1997, only Audi was shod with Dunlop rubber; all the rest were on Michelins. In Japan, though, Bridgestone and Toyo are also in evidence.

Advertising

The BTCC likes to be seen as a wholesome family affair. Unlike many countries, the organizers don't allow the advertising of tobacco or tobacco products in any form, and this extends to products not permitted on British TV.

Garlanded Donington race winner Tim Harvey lets success go to his head while 1991 Champ Will Hoy takes a more sober view: their racewear proclaims their major sponsors, Labatt's brewery.

Alfa Romeo 155TS Silverstone

CHASSIS: Abarth-prepared seam-welded four-door Alfa 155 monocoque, stiffened by tubular steel roll cage; left-hand drive

ENGINE: Abarth-built water-cooled, in-line, four-cylinder, dry-sump DOHC 16-valve unit, transverse location, canted rearwards at 27 degrees. TAG 3.8 multi-point sequential and programmable fuel injection. Digital electronic ignition. Cast-iron block from Alfa 164 Turbo, aluminium alloy head from 4WD 155. Bore/stroke: 86mm x 86mm = 1998cc

POWER OUTPUT: 280bhp at 8500rpm

TRANSMISSION: front-wheel drive, Hewland six-speed sequential gearbox. AP hydraulic racing clutch, solid steel driveshafts, limited slip differential

SUSPENSION: McPherson struts at front, trailing links at rear, with coil springs, gas-pressurized Bilstein dampers and heavy-duty hubs

BRAKING SYSTEM: Brembo racing calipers, eight-piston front, four-piston rear, with 15in ventilated front discs, solid rear discs. Carbon metallic pads

FUEL CELL: single, rear mounted beneath floor, 70-litres

STEERING: power-assisted rack and pinion

WHEELS: Speedline-cast MIM, 18in x 8.25in

TYRES: Michelin

WEIGHT: 975kg

WHEELBASE: 2540mm

TRACK: front: 1490mm, rear: 1490mm

LENGTH: 4487mm

WIDTH: 1717mm

HEIGHT: 1400mm

Audi A4 Quattro

CHASSIS: standard A4 Quattro, seam-welded, steel roll cage welded in; dual-circuit fire extinguisher system, Recaro seat, left-hand drive, six-point Sabelt harness

ENGINE: four-cylinder, water-cooled, in-line, longitudinal installation, 16-valve dry-sump unit, developed by Audi Sport; alloy block, alloy head. Bosch Motronic Mp 2.8 ignition and induction system; closed loop three-way catalytic converter. Bore: 85mm x stroke: 88mm = 1998cc; oil capacity: 5.5 litres Castrol fully synthetic engine oil

POWER OUTPUT: 296bhp at 8250rpm

TRANSMISSION: permanent four-wheel drive, Torsen centre differential, viscous locking front diff, multi-plate rear diff. Löbrö homokinetic three-arm sliding universal jointed half shafts Sequential Audi six-speed sport gearbox. Single dry-plate carbon fibre clutch

SUSPENSION: independent front and rear by double wishbones, adjustable gas dampers, coil springs, anti-roll bar

BRAKING SYSTEM: continuously adjustable by driver; hydraulic dual-circuit, four-piston calipers; Alcon-ventilated steel discs, 343mm x 32mm front, 330mm x 28mm rear diameter; asbestos-free pads

FUEL CELL: FT3 FIA-spec safety tank, 100-litres

STEERING: power-assisted rack and pinion

WHEELS: O.Z. forged aluminium alloy, 19in x 8.2in

TYRES: Dunlop radial, 215/650 R19

WEIGHT: 1040kg (without ballast)

WHEELBASE: 2610mm

LENGTH: 4479mm

WIDTH: 1753mm

HEIGHT: 1311mm

BMW 320i

CHASSIS: seam-welded four-door, left-hand-drive monocoque, 40 metres of tubular roll cage welded-in; flame-retardant-clad Kevlar racing seat with integral head protection

ENGINE: BMW Motorsport-developed S42 four-cylinder in-line, longitudinal installation, 16-valve, DOHC, dry-sump unit. Iron block, alloy head. Bore/stroke: 86.5mm x 85.0mm = 1998cc. Double-spark ignition coil, oil/water heat exchanger, BMW ECU, metal-based catalytic converter and oxygen sensor

POWER OUTPUT: 298bhp at 8300rpm

TRANSMISSION: rear-wheel drive, six-speed Holinger sequential gearbox, multi-plate limited slip differential, final drive ratio: 4.37:1; two-plate carbon fibre clutch

SUSPENSION: front: single-pivot McPherson strut with castor offset; small positive kingpin offset, lateral force compensation. Rear: central-arm axle with semi-trailing arm and double transverse link

BRAKING SYSTEM: hydraulically operated dual-circuit, vented discs, 345mm x 32mm front, 280mm x 25.4mm rear; Brembo 8-piston calipers front, 4-piston calipers rear

FUEL CELL: carbon fibre

STEERING: rack and pinion

WHEELS: BMW magnesium alloy 19in x 8.3in

TYRES: Michelin 215/650 x 19

WEIGHT: 1000kg (without ballast)

WHEELBASE: 2700mm

LENGTH: 4433mm

WIDTH: 1698mm

HEIGHT: 1270mm

Ford Mondeo Ghia

CHASSIS: Reynard-built seam-welded, five-door, left-hand-drive Mondeo monocoque, tubular roll cage welded-in

ENGINE: Cosworth-developed six-cylinder 60 degree Vee, transverse installation, canted rearwards. 24-valve, DOHC, dry-sump unit. Alloy block, alloy head. Bore/stroke: 2000cc Bosch engine management system, Duckhams lubrication

POWER OUTPUT: 295bhp at 8500rpm

TRANSMISSION: front-wheel drive, six-speed Reynard-Xtrac sequential gearbox, transverse mounting. Limited slip differential, two-plate carbon fibre clutch

SUSPENSION: front: McPherson strut located by two-piece lower wishbone, cockpit adjustable anti-roll bar. Rear: McPherson strut located by parallel arms and forward link, plus cockpit adjustable anti-roll bar; coil springs and Penske gas dampers all round

BRAKING SYSTEM: hydraulically operated dual-circuit system, AP Racing ventilated discs, 380mm front, 305mm rear; 6-piston calipers front, 2-piston calipers rear. Carbon metallic pads

FUEL CELL: carbon fibre

STEERING: rack and pinion

WHEELS: O.Z. forged magnesium alloy 19in x 8in

TYRES: Michelin 215/650 x 19

WEIGHT: 975kg

WHEELBASE: 2704mm

LENGTH: 4481mm

WIDTH: 1749mm

HEIGHT: 1425mm

Honda Accord 2.0i LS

CHASSIS: Prodrive-built, seam-welded, four-door, right-hand-drive Accord monocoque, welded-in tubular roll cage

ENGINE: Neil Brown Engineering-developed four-cylinder in-line, transverse installation, 16-valve, DOHC, dry-sump unit. Alloy block, alloy head. Bore/stroke: 1998cc EFI engine management system, TBC Fuel system

POWER OUTPUT: 325bhp at 8500rpm

TRANSMISSION: front-wheel drive, six-speed Hewland sequential gearbox, transverse mounting. Limited slip diff with laminar and viscous options; 5.5in twin-plate carbon fibre clutch

SUSPENSION: front: double wishbones, anti-roll bar. Rear: multilink double wishbones, anti-roll bar; coil springs and Bilstein gas dampers all round

BRAKING SYSTEM: hydraulically assisted dual-circuit system, AP Racing ventilated discs, 355mm front, 275mm rear; 4-piston calipers front, 2-piston calipers rear. Carbon metallic pads

FUEL CELL: FIA-spec carbon fibre

STEERING: manual or power-assisted rack and pinion

WHEELS: O.Z. Racing magnesium alloy 19in x 8.20in

TYRES: Michelin 215/650 x 19

WEIGHT: 975kg

WHEELBASE: 2720mm

LENGTH: 4685mm

WIDTH: 1720mm

HEIGHT: 1380mm

Nissan Primera

CHASSIS: RouseSport-prepared seam-welded four-door Primera monocoque, stiffened by tubular steel roll cage; right-hand drive

ENGINE: RouseSport-built water-cooled, in-line, four-cylinder, dry-sump DOHC 16-valve unit, transverse location, reverse-head layout. Alloy block, alloy head. Bore x stroke: 88mm x 82mm = 1998cc. Compression ratio: 12:1. JECS fuel injection, JECS electronic ignition and engine management. HJS catalyst exhaust system

POWER OUTPUT: 300bhp at 8500rpm

TRANSMISSION: front-wheel-drive, transverse-mounted Hewland 6-speed sequential gearbox. 3-plate carbon fibre clutch, limited slip differential

SUSPENSION: wishbones at front with ARE cockpit adjustable anti-roll bar; McPherson struts at rear with ARE cockpit adjustable anti-roll bar; coil springs and gas-pressurized dampers all round

BRAKING SYSTEM: hydraulic dual-circuit system; Brembo 6-piston calipers front, AP Racing 2-piston calipers rear, with 15in ventilated front, solid rear discs. Carbon metallic pads

FUEL CELL: carbon fibre FIA-spec

STEERING: power-assisted rack and pinion with electric pressure pump

WHEELS: Dymag 19in x 8in

TYRES: Michelin Pilot

WEIGHT: 975kg

WHEELBASE: 2540mm

TRACK: front: 1473mm, rear: 1461mm

LENGTH: 4394mm

WIDTH: 1700mm

HEIGHT: 1346mm

Peugeot 406 ST

CHASSIS: Peugeot Sport-prepared seam-welded four-door 406 monocoque, stiffened by tubular steel roll cage; left-hand drive; spoiler kit includes front skirt and rear spoiler

ENGINE: Peugeot Sport-developed XU9J4 Evolution 8, water-cooled, in-line, four-cylinder, dry-sump DOHC 16-valve unit, transverse location to rear of engine bay. Alloy block, alloy head. Bore x stroke: 86mm x 86mm = 1998cc. Compression ratio: 13:1. Fuel system: Marelli MR1 injection; ignition: 4-coil static; Weber-Marelli engine management system

POWER OUTPUT: 300bhp at 8300rpm

TRANSMISSION: front-wheel drive, transverse-mounted Xtrac six-speed sequential gearbox, column change. 2-plate carbon fibre clutch, limited slip differential with laminar and viscous options located ahead of engine

SUSPENSION: McPherson struts at front with anti-roll bar; multi-link trailing arm with torsion bars at rear with anti-roll bar; Faulkner coil springs and WP gas-pressurized dampers

BRAKING SYSTEM: hydraulic dual-circuit system; Brembo 8-piston calipers front, Alcon 4-piston calipers rear, 380mm ventilated front, 280mm solid rear discs. Carbon metallic pads

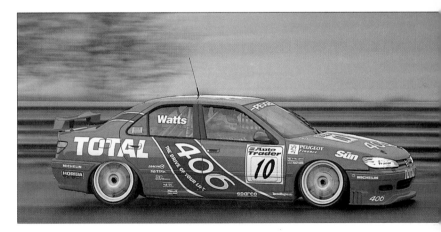

FUEL CELL: carbon fibre FIA-spec, 50-litres

STEERING: power-assisted rack and pinion

WHEELS: Tecnomagnesio 7-spoke 19 x 8.25in

TYRES: Michelin 215/650 x 19

WEIGHT: 975kg, split front/rear: 58/42

WHEELBASE: 2668mm

TRACK: front: 1540mm, rear: 1530mm

LENGTH: 4546mm

WIDTH: 1752mm

HEIGHT: 1240mm

Renault Laguna 2.0 RT

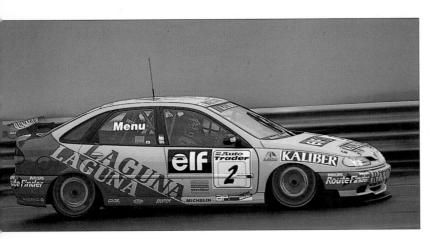

CHASSIS: Williams Touring Car Engineering-built, seam-welded, five-door, left-hand-drive Laguna monocoque, welded-in tubular roll cage. Sparco/Williams carbon-epoxy seat, suede covering; 6-point Sabelt harness, Sparco steering wheel

ENGINE: Moteurs Sodemo-prepared four-cylinder in-line, transverse installation, 16-valve, DOHC, dry-sump unit, Elf lubrication. Iron block, alloy head. Bore/stroke: 1998cc Magneti Marelli engine system, Williams data-logging system. Single water radiator with oil/water heat exchanger

POWER OUTPUT: 285bhp at 8500rpm

TRANSMISSION: front-wheel drive, six-speed Williams-Hewland sequential gearbox, transverse mounting. Limited slip differential; 3-plate carbon fibre clutch

SUSPENSION: front: McPherson struts, anti-roll bar. Rear: trailing arm, torsion bar, anti-roll bar; coil springs and gas-filled dampers all round

BRAKING SYSTEM: hydraulically assisted dual-circuit system, AP Racing ventilated discs front, 378mm, AP drilled discs rear, 255mm; 6-piston calipers front, 4-piston calipers rear. Carbon metallic pads

FUEL CELL: FIA-spec carbon fibre; 3.375-litre fire extinguisher system in carbon bottle

STEERING: power-assisted rack and pinion

WHEELS: O.Z. Racing 19in x 8.3in

TYRES: Michelin 215/650 x 19

WEIGHT: 975kg

WHEELBASE: 2670mm

LENGTH: 4508mm

WIDTH: 1752mm

HEIGHT: 1433mm

TRACK: front, 1525mm; rear, 1490mm

Toyota Carina E

CHASSIS: TOM'S-developed, seam-welded, four-door, right-hand-drive Carina monocoque, welded-in tubular roll cage

ENGINE: TOM'S-developed four-cylinder in-line, transverse installation, 16-valve, DOHC, dry-sump unit. Cast iron block, alloy head. Bore x stroke: 86mm x 86mm = 1988cc. Compression ratio: 14:1; Zytec engine management system

POWER OUTPUT: 300bhp at 8500rpm

TRANSMISSION: front-wheel-drive, six-speed Xtrac sequential gearbox, transverse mounting. Limited slip differential; 3-plate sintered clutch

SUSPENSION: front: Toyota 'super-strut', anti-roll bar. Rear: McPherson strut, anti-roll bar; coil springs and gas-filled dampers all round

BRAKING SYSTEM: hydraulically assisted dual-circuit system, Brembo ventilated steel discs, 355mm front, 275mm rear; twin 8-piston calipers front, 4-piston calipers rear. Carbon metallic pads

FUEL CELL: FIA-spec carbon fibre

STEERING: power-assisted rack and pinion

WHEELS: O.Z. Racing 19in x 8.3in

TYRES: Dunlop 215/650 x 19

WEIGHT: 975kg

WHEELBASE: 2580mm

LENGTH: 4530mm

WIDTH: 1695mm

HEIGHT: 1410mm

TRACK: front, rear: 1455mm

Vauxhall Vectra

CHASSIS: Triple-Eight (888)-built four-door, left-hand drive Vectra monocoque, welded-in tubular roll cage

ENGINE: Swindon Racing Engines-developed 4-cylinder in-line, transverse installation, 16-valve, DOHC, dry-sump unit, Mobil lubrication. Alloy block, alloy head. Bore/stroke: 88mm x 85mm = 1988cc. Compression ratio: 13.0:1 Motec M4 engine management system, stainless steel exhaust system

POWER OUTPUT: 295bhp at 8500rpm

TRANSMISSION: front-wheel drive, six-speed Xtrac sequential gearbox, transverse mounting. Limited slip differential with laminar and viscous options; 3-plate sintered clutch

SUSPENSION: front: racing design McPherson struts, lightweight lower wishbones, rocker-activated tubular steel anti-roll bar. Rear: twin lateral links coupled to aerospace-spec steel trailing arm; tubular steel anti-roll bar; coaxial coil springs and gas dampers all round

BRAKING SYSTEM: hydraulically assisted dual-circuit system, AP Racing ventilated discs, 340mm front, twin 6-piston calipers; 240mm solid discs rear, 2-piston calipers. Carbon metallic pads

FUEL CELL: 60-litre carbon fibre under rear seat platform

STEERING: high ratio power-assisted rack and pinion

WHEELS: O.Z. Racing forged magnesium alloy 19in x 9in

TYRES: Michelin

WEIGHT: 975kg

WHEELBASE: 2640mm

LENGTH: 4477mm

WIDTH: 1707mm

HEIGHT: 1310mm

TRACK: front, 1484mm; rear, 1470mm

Volvo 850

CHASSIS: TWR-built, seam-welded, four-door, right-hand-drive 850 GLT monocoque, welded-in tubular roll cage; TWR front splitter, rear wing to FIA spec; flame-retardant clad Kevlar racing seat with integral head protection; Momo Corse steering wheel

ENGINE: TWR-tuned Volvo Motorsport five-cylinder in-line, transverse installation, 20-valve, DOHC, dry-sump unit. Alloy block, alloy head. Bore/stroke: 83mm x 73.9mm = 1999cc. TWR data-logging system

POWER OUTPUT: 290bhp at 8500rpm

TRANSMISSION: front-wheel drive, six-speed Xtrac sequential gearbox, transverse mounting. Limited slip differential; 3-plate carbon fibre clutch

SUSPENSION: front: TWR-fabricated McPherson struts, Ohlins gas damper units, anti-roll bar. Rear: Volvo Delta-link, semi-independent trailing arms, anti-roll bar; coil springs and Ohlins gas dampers

BRAKING SYSTEM: hydraulically assisted dual circuit system, ventilated discs, 355mm front, 270mm rear; AP balanced braking system, AP 8-piston calipers front, Brembo 2-piston calipers rear. Carbon metallic pads

FUEL CELL: Premier rubber safety cell contained in carbon/kevlar tray

STEERING: TWR power-assisted rack and pinion, TWR 90-degree bevel box

WHEELS: BBS forged magnesium alloy, 19in x 8.20in

TYRES: Michelin 215/650 x 19

WEIGHT: 975kg

WHEELBASE: 2670mm

LENGTH: 4670mm

WIDTH: 1760mm

HEIGHT: 1430mm

The Drivers

Competitors in the BTCC come from a variety of racing backgrounds and bring their own brand of skills to play in this test of nerve, racecraft and car control. Success depends on commitment, ambition, ruthlessness and a good deal of luck.

Some drivers are perennial tin-top specialists, others are exiles from single-seaters and sports-GT racing, while a few are young chargers using Super Touring as a rung on their way to stardom.

Occasionally we find a Grand Prix star for whom all the doors have closed at the pinnacle of the sport, although Formula 1 exiles are more common in European Super Touring and the ITC World series than the BTCC.

A career in the big-time doesn't necessarily mean instant Touring Car success, though. Of the ex-F1 drivers to feature in the UK, Derek Warwick and Julian Bailey made rather less of an impact on the BTCC than Gabriele Tarquini and Jo Winkelhock, while Nigel Mansell's much publicized one-off TOCA drive showed a great deal of promise, but ultimately demonstrated that Touring Cars require a very different kind of car control to that demonstrated in Formula 1.

There has always been an element of crossover between European and British touring car racing, and some drivers, such as Steve Soper and Roberto Ravaglia,

Tin-top wizard John Cleland provides an exotic shower for the fans after winning both races in the 1995 Donington double-header.

Some you lose, some you win: Jo Winkelhock looks grim after a crash at Snetterton in 1996, but it was a prelude to winning the second race.

continue to pursue their careers in Germany or Japan as well as making their mark on the UK circuit. Others tend to drift in and out of the BTCC according to sponsorship or team commitments. Some drivers, like John Cleland, are keen to participate in far-flung events like the Toohey's Bathurst classic in Australia, while Aussie legend Peter 'Perfect' Brock decided in 1996 that Super Touring was the way to go, confirming the category's global appeal.

Whatever their background, the drivers whose potted biographies are listed here have at some time made their mark in the BTCC. While the majority are professionals with contracts with works or works-backed teams, a minority are privateers running in the potentially lucrative Total Cup section. While on-track rivalries are intense, and occasionally manifest between team-mates, the majority of BTCC drivers enjoy a degree of camaraderie quite as high as in any other category of the sport.

Some of these men reached the heights of Touring Car success almost from the moment they entered the sport. Others have given their all year after year with little tangible reward. The bravery and courage of each one of them has helped make Touring Car racing one of the world's most exhilarating and exceptional sports.

Jeff Allam

Jeff is something of a veteran in racing terms, having made his mark back in 1978 with a 3.0-litre Capri, finishing second in class in the BTCC that year. He placed second in the 3000 class again in 1979, and won the division in 1982 with a Rover SD1.

Claims to fame in the mid-1980s included winning the daunting Bathurst 1000 with a Rover Vitesse in 1984, and the Silverstone TT in 1986 in a TWR Rover. A change of category in 1989 saw Jeff participating in the inaugural TVR Tuscan Challenge. These sportscars were powered by basically the same engine as the SD1, and Allam went on to scoop the Tuscan title.

In 1992 Jeff took two wins in the Cavalier in the BTCC. In 1994 he was 10th overall. In 1995 he raced in Australian Super Touring with a Mondeo, coming seventh overall with a best race result of third. Future assaults on the Bathurst 1000 and Australian Super Touring were on the cards for the man chosen by TOCA as Arbiter of Driving Standards in the BTCC. Allam's 92.6 per cent finishing record remains but privateer Richard Kaye is close, finishing 92 per cent of races he enters.

Gary Ayles

Like most ambitious young drivers, Gary started out in Formula Ford 1600, and within a year had finished fourth in the UK's national series, and earned the LEP Young Driver of the Year award. He took second place in the BBC TV Grandstand Trophy for FF2000, and graduated to Formula 3 for 1987. He went for the one-make Formula Vauxhall-Lotus series in 1988, and fourth place in the championship was good enough to justify a move back to Formula 3 with Jack Brabham Racing.

Gary's first taste of the BTCC was in 1991, when he was a works Toyota driver alongside Andy Rouse in the RouseSport-prepared Carinas. There followed a three-year stint as works Peugeot driver in the Italian Superturismo series, and he finished the 1992 season in second place. His season in the BTCC with RouseSport Primeras consisted mostly of tail end finishes plus a couple of accidents – a legacy chiefly of the car's current lack of development rather than any deficiency in Ayles' considerable talents. Gary is a senior instructor at Brands Hatch racing school, which gives him a head start at BTCC rounds there.

Race History

Born: 19 December 1954, Epsom, Surrey
Lives: Epsom

1978: 2nd in class, British Saloon Car Championship (Capri)
1982: 1st in class, British Saloon Car Championship (Rover)
1984: 1st, Bathurst 1000 (Rover)
1986: 1st, Tourist Trophy (Rover)
1989: 1st, TVR Tuscan Challenge
1994: 10th, BTCC (Vauxhall Cavalier)
1995: 7th, Australian Super Touring series (Ford Mondeo)
1996: Arbiter of BTCC

Race History

Born: 25 September 1965, Crawley
Lives: Robertsbridge, Sussex

1986: 4th, RAC Formula Ford 1600 Championship; 2nd, BBC Grandstand FF2000 Championship
1987: British Formula 3 Championship
1989: British F3 series (Jack Brabham Racing)
1991: BTCC, (RouseSport Toyota Carina)
1992: 2nd, Italian Superturismo (Peugeot)
1996: BTCC (Rouse-Sport Nissan Primera)

Julian Bailey

Another driver with his roots originally in single-seaters – and who once attained the dizzy heights of Formula 1, Julian spent five seasons in the BTCC between 1991 and 1995. He started off with Nissan, quickly transferring to Toyota to race the Carina. He ended the 1993 season in fifth place, having scored one victory. The following year was less good, with 12th place overall, but he made a slight improvement in 1995 at ninth spot in the final Championship standings, with a fourth place his best result.

Julian had also raced, with success, in New Zealand and South Africa. He achieved high placings in the Dave Cook-built Toyota Camry in South Africa in 1996, including a win at Killarney in July, and looked set for a return to the BTCC.

His career began in Formula Ford, and he won the 1982 Formula Ford Festival. By 1987 he was up in F3000, and he won at Brands in a Lola-Cosworth. A promising talent in single-seaters, he was given his F1 chance by Ken Tyrrell, and drove in seven Grands Prix for the Tyrrell and Lotus teams between 1988 and 1991.

John Bintcliffe

New to the BTCC in 1996, and indeed to racing of any kind at this level, John acquitted himself with dignity when there were plenty of people who thought they had a better claim on the number two seat at Audi. Bintcliffe's selection for the plumb Audi job was based on nothing more than a couple of seasons racing Renault Clios – in which he was Elf Renault Clio Cup UK Champion in 1994 with five race wins, and a successful season with the BIM team in the Ford Credit Fiesta Trophy series which saw him become champion with six victories. But one-make racing is notoriously cut-throat competitive, and to win in two consecutive years says a lot about a driver's tenacity and skill.

Bintcliffe's fairy-tale elevation to the BTCC ranks was a result of his second place in a one-off Porsche race at Snetterton. It led to a discussion with Audi's BTCC co-ordinator Richard Lloyd, who was moved to offer him a season driving the A4. Although the choice of an inexperienced number two for Biela was a logical one, with Bintcliffe unlikely to challenge him for title honours, the Yorkshireman gave a very good account of himself.

Race History

Born: 9 October 1961, Woolwich, London

1982: 1st, Formula Ford Festival
1984: 2nd, British FF2000 Championship
1987: British F3000 series
1989: World Sportscar Championship (Nissan)
1991: BTCC (Nissan, Toyota)
1993: 5th, BTCC (Toyota Carina)
1994: 1st, Pukekohe 500; 12th, BTCC (Toyota Carina)
1995: 9th, BTCC (Toyota Carina)

Race History

Born: 7 February 1966, Bridlington, North Yorkshire
Lives: Harrogate, North Yorkshire

1992: 5th, Honda CRX Championship
1993: 6th, Renault Elf Oils Clio Championship
1994: 1st, Renault Elf Oils Clio Championship
1995: 1st, Ford Credit Fiesta Championship
1996: 7th, BTCC (Audi A4 Quattro)
1997: BTCC (Audi A4 Quattro)

Frank Biela

Twice runner-up in the German DTM series – his lead scuttled in the last round by barging Bimmers – Frank opened his account in the BTCC with towering performances in the four-wheel-drive Audi.

Frank has been very much to the forefront of Audi's rise to prominence in touring car racing, but his grounding was in single-seaters. He started out racing karts in 1982, switching to Formula Fords in 1984; he was second in the German national series in 1986. The following year he scored one win driving a Sierra XR4 in the German Touring Car Championship, reverting to single-seaters in 1988, and coming a creditable third in the German Formula 3 Championship.

Back in saloons in 1990, he topped the podium once with a Mercedes 190E. He took the German Touring Car title in 1991 in a works 2.5-litre Class 1 Audi V8 Quattro. There was only one win in 1992, when he was driving for Audi in German Class 1 races and contesting the 2.0-litre class in France with the Audi 80 Quattro, but he took the overall honours the following year in the French Supertourisme Championship. In 1994 Frank was

Race History

Born: 2 August 1964, Neuss, Germany
Lives: Marienbad and Monaco

1986: 2nd, German FF2000 Championship
1988: 3rd, German Formula 3 Championship
1991: 1st, German Touring Car Championship
1993: 1st, French Championship
1995: 1st, Touring Car World Cup (Audi A4 Quattro)
1996: BTCC Champion (Audi A4 Quattro)
1997: BTCC (Audi A4 Quattro)

second in the ADAC Tourenwagen Cup with the Audi; in Italy he won two rounds of the Superturismo series.

With four wins out of eight rounds during the 1995 season, he came third in the ADAC Super Touring category in the Audi A4, and won two other important races with it – the AA Fleetcar race at Kyalami, South Africa, and FIA's Touring Car World Cup at Paul Ricard.

Frank started the 1996 BTCC season as favourite. A mid-season back operation reduced his pace, but he took the title at Thruxton in August. Reduction of the A4's weight penalty midway through 1997 saw Frank's championship defense improve considerably.

Frank Biela was in masterful form when winning the 1996 BTCC in his Audi A4 Quattro.

Kelvin Burt

With eight wins in the 1988 British Formula Ford Championship, Kelvin was clearly destined for a successful career in motor sport. Single-seaters looked the way for him to go, and he spent the next six years climbing the ladder. In 1989 he was second in the British FF series, and the following year took just one win in the Formula Vauxhall-Lotus Challenge. Seven victories in 1991 brought him the Vauxhall-Lotus title, and in 1992 he graduated to Formula 3 with a Reynard-Mugen. He won the Championship in 1993 in a Paul Stewart Racing Dallara-Mugen.

He was employed as test driver by the Jordan F1 team in 1994, and in 1995 for the Ligier F1 team, and had his BTCC debut at season's end in a RouseSport Mondeo. For 1995 Kelvin replaced the retiring Andy Rouse, taking his place alongside Paul Radisich in the Ford Mondeo. He won one race out of 23 – at Snetterton – with one fastest lap to his credit. Kelvin also took a trip to Macau to win the Guia touring car race for Toyota. He partnered Swede Rickard Rydell in the TWR Volvo 850 in 1996, and the S40 in 1997.

Lee Brookes

A newcomer to the BTCC in 1996, Lee bought one of the ex-works Toyota Carinas and with back-up from all-round Toyota competition specialists TOM'S, played himself in with some gritty drives among the privateers in the Total Cup division.

He was senior British kart champion in 1990, switching to cars and the Renault Clio Challenge in 1993. He was fourth in the points standings that year, and improved in 1994 to third place. Seven first places and three seconds in Clios in 1995 won him the title, as well as earning him the opportunity of a test drive in a works Laguna.

In winning the 1996 Total Cup he was a regular finisher, albeit at the bottom end of the field, although he came a creditable 10th at Thruxton in round five. With four Total Cup wins in 1996, Brookes's Toyota was plagued with power understeer for much of the season, the main reason being lack of baseline data for setting up the Carina, coupled with a tight budget. For 1997, Lee defended his Total Cup honours with an ex-works Peugeot 406.

Race History

Born: 7 September 1967, Birmingham
Lives: Tamworth, Staffordshire

1991: 1st, Vauxhall-Lotus Championship for John Village Automotive
1993: 1st, British F3 Championship (Paul Stewart Racing Reynard)
1994: Test driver, Jordan Grand Prix; 2nd, Macau F3 race
1995: 8th, BTCC (Ford Mondeo)
1996: 11th, BTCC (Volvo 850)
1997: BTCC (Volvo S40)

Race History

Born: 22 February 1968, Walsall, Staffordshire
Lives: Willenhall, Staffordshire

1990: Senior British kart champion
1993: 4th, Renault Elf Oils Clio Championship
1994: 3rd, Renault Elf Oils Clio Championship
1995: 1st, Renault Elf Oils Clio Championship
1996: 1st, BTCC Total Cup (Toyota Carina)
1997: BTCC Total Cup (Peugeot)

John Cleland

Tin-top racing's most enduring star, John Cleland has twice been BTCC Champion. He achieved the goal first in 1989 with his Class-winning 16-valve Astra GTE, and took the crown once more in 1995, driving the Cavalier in its final year of competition.

He's always raced General Motors products. John was Thundersaloon champ in 1987 and 1988 in a highly modified Vauxhall Senator, and again in 1989 with a Carlton. Shunning the dramatic excesses of horsepower in Thundersaloons, he drove the Astra in the BTCC the same year; the start of the second phase of his career. In 1990, the inaugural year of the Cavalier, he took three Class victories and was runner-up in the series, accomplishing the same result in 1991. There were three victories in 1992, as well as the conquest of the TOCA

John Cleland took the BTCC crown for the second time in 1995 with the ageing Cavalier.

Race History

Born: 15 July 1952, Wishaw, Scotland	**1991:** 2nd, BTCC (Vauxhall Cavalier)
Lives: Galashiels, Scotland	**1993:** 4th, BTCC (Vauxhall Cavalier)
	1994: 4th, BTCC (Vauxhall Cavalier)
1986: 1st, Thunder-saloon Championship	**1995:** 1st, BTCC (Vauxhall Cavalier)
1989: 1st, BTCC (Vauxhall Astra GTE)	**1996:** 8th, BTCC (Vauxhall Vectra)
1990: 2nd, BTCC (Vauxhall Cavalier)	**1997:** BTCC (Vectra)

Shootout. John was third in the BTCC that year. Only one win came in 1993 but he managed to come fourth in the Drivers' title.

In amongst the Alfas, Fords and BMWs, there were two BTCC race wins in 1994. He was now using the Ray Mallock-prepared Cavalier, and John was fourth in the title race, albeit first British driver. But for 1995, everything came good, and with six wins, five seconds and seven third places, John was BTCC Champion, handsomely beating Menu and Rydell for the title. It was a tough act to follow, especially with the untried Vectra, but there were some high placings in 1996 and 1977.

Johnny Cecotto

The brilliant Venezuelan rider made his name on the world motorcycle stage in 1975 and, in common with Surtees and Hailwood before him, took to four wheels like a natural.

In 1982 he was second in the European Formula 2 Championship in a March-BMW, and during the next two years drove in 18 Grands Prix for Teddy Yip's Theodore team and for Toleman, where Ayrton Senna got started. He progressed no further in Formula 1, and instead moved into touring cars. In 1986, Cecotto drove the highly successful Volvo 240T in the European series, taking two wins. The following year he had four victories in the World Touring Car Championship in a BMW M3, and in 1988 he campaigned a Mercedes 190E in the German Touring Car series.

Thereafter he drove only BMWs, winning the Italian title in 1989 with seven victories in an M3, followed by a four-year run of successes in the German series. Johnny partnered David Brabham in 1995 for the BTCC assault, but the cars were afflicted with problems and he was placed 12th in the final results.

Race History

Born: 20 January 1956, Caracas, Venezuela

1975: 1st, World 350cc Motorcycle Championship (Yamaha)
1982: 2nd, European Formula 2 Championship (March-BMW)

1989: 1st, Italian Touring Car Championship (BMW M3)
1990: 2nd, German Touring Car Championship (BMW M3)
1993: 1st, German ADAC GT Cup (BMW M3 GTr)
1995: 12th, BTCC (BMW 318is)

Robb Gravett

In the late 1980s and early 1990s it was looking good for Robb Gravett. He was masterful in the awesomely fast Cosworth RS500 and was BTCC champ in 1990. But when the formula changed in 1991 and excluded the turbo cars, Robb's fortunes dipped.

His career began in the early 1980s and he was Class A Champion in 1987 in a Sierra. Pitching into the hurly-burly of the BTCC in 1988, Robb emerged runner-up in the title fight. His Championship year included seven consecutive race wins in the RS500, and there were nine victories in total out of 13 rounds in 1990, plus seven fastest laps.

Following the glory years, Gravett drove a Sapphire in 1991, followed by a Peugeot Mi16 in 1992 and 1993. He reappeared for the 1994 finale with a Mondeo, bent on doing a full season in 1995. It was not to be, although he made a mid-season comeback, finishing third at Snetterton – the best ever result by a privateer.

For 1996, Robb was driving Mondeos for Team Dynamics, and in 1997, a Graham Hathaway-prepared Honda Accord.

Race History

Born: 2 May 1956, London
Lives: Berkshire

1984: 1st, MG Owners' Club Trophy
1987: 1st, British Production Saloons
1989: 2nd, BTCC (Sierra Cosworth RS500)
1990: 1st, BTCC (Sierra Cosworth RS500)
1991: BTCC (Sierra Sapphire)
1992: BTCC (Peugeot 405 Mi16)
1995: 20th, BTCC (Ford Mondeo)
1996: BTCC (Ford Mondeo)
1997: BTCC (Honda Accord)

Tim Harvey

Tim's career began in karts in 1979 and he won the 1981 National 100cc title. He forsook karts for Formula Fords in 1983, and won a total of 12 FF1600 races driving a Van Diemen in his first year. He drove in the MG Metro Challenge during both 1984 and 1985, broke both ankles in a crash at Silverstone, and was out of action for a year.

His comeback was in a mighty Rover Vitesse, and he took Class A in the British Touring Car series. A change of category found him driving a Tiga in the British Sports Car Championship, which he won, and he also competed in the World Sportscar series with a Spice. Between 1989 and 1990 he drove one of the ubiquitous RS500s in the BTCC. The Cossie's knockabout handling was well suited to Tim; he finished third in Class A in 1990.

For 1991 he joined the Vic Lee Motorsport team and gained one BTCC victory in a BMW M3. Running new 318s in the 1992 series, he won the Championship with

a run of six race wins. He transferred to the Renault squad for 1993, and for the next two seasons drove the R19 and Laguna. He knotched up the R19's maiden BTCC victory, and he came ninth in the 1994 series with one win in the Laguna.

Tim's fortunes were to improve considerably during 1995 when he drove the TWR Volvo 850, and there were two wins for him at Brands Hatch, which took him to fifth overall in the Championship.

Another shift of allegiances led him to Total Team Peugeot for the 1996 series, but, in common with his colleague Patrick Watts, Tim found it hard going in the midfield order. 1997 saw a marked improvement.

Race History

Born: 20 November 1961, Farnborough
Lives: Oxfordshire

1981: 1st, National 100cc Kart Championship
1987: 1st, BTCC Class A (Rover Vitesse)
1988: 1st, British Sports Car Championship (Tiga)
1992: 1st, BTCC (BMW 318is)
1994: 9th, BTCC (Renault Laguna)
1995: 5th, BTCC (Volvo 850)
1996: 15th, BTCC (Peugeot 406)
1997: BTCC (Peugeot 406)

Will Hoy

At 43, Will Hoy ranks as an old hand in motor sport, having spent much of the 1970s racing karts, where he won numerous events, including a Class title in the 1979 World Cup.

The Clubman's Formula is the province of back-to-basics sports racers, who enjoy some of the best camaraderie in the paddock. It was here that Will began his rise to fame. He was to capture three successive Clubman's titles, between 1982 and 1984, and he also competed in a number of Thundersaloon events for good measure.

In 1985 Will competed in the World Endurance Championship in a Tiga, setting a new lap record for C2 class cars at the Brands Hatch 1000km (625 miles). That year he also raced for Daihatsu in the British Production Saloons series. For 1986 he took in the World Sportscar Championship, the All-Japan Sportscar Championship and Thundersports, driving a Tiga-Hart and a Lola T286. There were also outings for Daihatsu in the UK Production Saloons series.

There was more sportscar racing for him during 1987, and Will took pole position for seven out of 10 World Championship events in an Argo-Zakspeed. He drove for TOM'S Toyota in the All-Japan series once more, and contested the Japanese Touring Car Championship. He was Class B champ with a works-backed BMW M3, and even managed to find time to race a Corolla in the BTCC.

Driving an M3 for Prodrive, Will raced in the 1988 European Touring Car series at the Silverstone and Donington rounds, and he was Class winner and second overall in the Japanese Touring Car Championship, again with an M3. On the World Sportscar scene, Will drove an Argo-Cosworth, sharing a Mazda for the Le Mans 24-Hours.

The VLM and Prodrive BMW M3s scorch away from the start at Silverstone in 1991.

Race History

Born: 2 April 1953, Melbourne, Cambridgeshire
Lives: Chelsea

1979: 1st, World Kart Class Champion
1987: 1st, Japanese Touring Car Championship Class B (BMW M3)
1990: 4th, Japanese Sportscar Championship (Porsche 962)
1991: 1st, BTCC (BMW M3)
1992: 2nd, BTCC (Toyota Carina)
1995: 4th, BTCC (Renault Laguna)
1996: 9th, BTCC (Renault Laguna)
1997: BTTC (Ford Mondeo)

His giddy schedule for 1989 took in the Nürburgring 24-Hours in a Prodrive BMW M3, a round of the BTCC and the complete Japanese Touring Car series. He enjoyed some high placings. He also shared a Porsche 962 with Vern Schuppan and Jean Alesi at Le Mans. The following year saw Hoy partnered with Stanley Dickens in a Porsche 962 for the Japanese Sportscar Championship and they ended the season fourth. Will raced a Jöest Porsche at Le Mans, and also competed in touring cars in Japan.

He became BTCC Champion in 1991, driving a Vic Lee Motorsport BMW M3 to three wins, four seconds and two third places. Will also ran in the Willhire 24-Hours, the TWR Jaguarsport XJR15 Challenge and the Japanese sportscar series. Moving on to Toyota Carinas alongside Andy Rouse for 1992, Will came second in the BTCC with two race wins and five second places. As well as being active in sportscars, he remained with Toyota for the next couple of years, but the TOM'S-built Carinas' fortunes were in decline.

Things started to perk up with Hoy's move to the Renault team to drive Lagunas alongside Alain Menu in 1995, and Will was placed fourth in the Championship thanks to his three wins and four second places.

The Williams-built Lagunas of 1996 grew steadily more able to match and sometimes beat the opposition, and although he was somewhat less spectacular than his Swiss team-mate, Will was always on the pace. For the 1977 season, Will transferred to Team Mondeo alongside Paul Radisich.

James Kaye

The elder of the two Kayes currently competing in the BTCC, James began karting in 1979. Between 1983 and 1990 he contested the British Production Saloon Car Championship in cars as diverse as the VW Golf GTi, the Cossie, the Saab 900 and the Honda CRX, winning the 1300cc class in 1984 and 1985 with a Vauxhall Nova. He took the 2.0-litre class in 1987 driving a Vauxhall Astra GTE, moving on the following year to the UK Renault 5 Turbo Cup series. He ended the season second and in 1989 was British Ford Fiesta Champion.

In 1991 there were two race wins in the standard British Group N series with a Honda CRX, and for 1992 James moved up into the BTCC, winning the TOCA Privateers' Cup with a Toyota Carina.

In 1993 his season was curtailed when the Toyota was gutted in a fire in the Knockhill paddock. However, James repeated his success of 1992 for the Maxted Toyota team in 1994. In 1995 James was joined by younger brother Richard in the BTCC.

He drove a Honda Accord in 1996 but, unlike his team-mate Leslie, he was never in contention for a win.

Richard Kaye

One of the front runners in the privateers' Total Cup division of the BTCC in 1995, Richard learned some useful lessons. He was runner-up in the 1995 Total Cup category, with three wins. For 1996, Richard was running the ex-Cleland Cavalier and was fastest of the privateers, but his 1996 season received an abrupt jolt when the Vauxhall got away from him on some oil at Oulton Park and pitched him into the barriers.

Richard had nine Total Cup wins by halfway through the 1996 season, and he was having to decide whether to scrap with BTCC works cars or simply hold station and drive for Total Cup points. He was relieved of 15 of these when disqualified at Brands for colliding with Steve Robertson's Mondeo. He was the only serious challenger to Lee Brookes for Total Cup honours.

His formative years were spent rallying. Turning to circuit racing in 1988 he was first in the St Helens Ford Championship in 1989 with a Fiesta XR2i. After a two-year lay-off, Richard returned in the British Ford Fiesta XR2 series in 1993. For 1997 Richard is Team Manager at Team Dynamics.

Race History

Born: 18 February 1964, Harrogate, Yorkshire
Lives: Hampshire

1984: 1st, Monroe and Uniroyal Production Saloon Car Championships, 2.0-litre Class (Vauxhall Nova)
1987: 1st, Uniroyal Production Saloons Championship (VW Golf GTi, Honda Civic Si)
1992: 1st, BTCC TOCA Privateers' Cup (Toyota Carina)
1994: 1st, BTCC TOCA Privateers' Cup (Toyota Carina)
1996: BTCC (Honda Accord)

Race History

Born: 30 September 1967, Harrogate, Yorkshire
Lives: Brighton

1988: 2nd, St Helens Ford Championship
1989: 1st, St Helens Ford Championship (Ford Fiesta)
1993: 4th, British Ford Fiesta Championship
1994: 2nd, British Ford Fiesta Championship
1995: 2nd, BTCC Total Cup (Ford Mondeo)
1996: 2nd, BTCC Total Cup (Vauxhall Cavalier)

David Leslie

David Leslie was Scottish Karting Champion five times up to 1976. He went into Formula Ford and won the BARC title in 1977, progressing to FF2000 to take the Shellsport Martini and Computercar titles in 1979. He was top Grovewood Award winner following his performance in the British Formula Atlantic series in 1980, and followed this up with a couple of seasons in Formula 3, even beating Ayrton Senna on one occasion.

He placed second in the C2 class in the 1987 World Sportscar Championship with the Ecosse. The next year he did Le Mans with Mazda and in 1989 and 1990 he was a member of the valiant Aston Martin team that contested the World Sportscar series.

In 1991, he was seen at two rounds of the BTCC, driving BMWs. For 1992 he drove a Vauxhall Cavalier for Ecurie Ecosse, finishing seventh overall, and eighth in 1993. He only completed half the 1994 season because Mazda pulled out due to inadequate budgets. Joint 10th in the 1995 BTCC in his first season with the MSD Honda Accord, it all came good for David when he topped the podium for Honda in 1996.

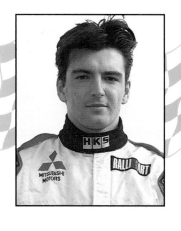

Owen McAuley

Owen has been a professional racing driver since he left school aged 17. He got started in motor racing with karts in the British Junior Championship in 1988, and in 1989 was Northern Ireland and All Ireland Junior Britain Kart Champion.

Between 1990 and 1992, he raced 100 National Karts and he was Northern Ireland Champion in 1990 and 1991. His real break came in 1993 when he raced Formula Vauxhall Lotus for the team named after one of his compatriots, Martin Donnelly Racing. The ex-Lotus Grand Prix driver had an eye for talent, and McAuley's potential was clear. In the winter series, Owen won two out of three F3 races driving for Paul Stewart Racing. He stayed with Paul Stewart to do Formula Vauxhall-Lotus in 1994, and emerged champion at season's end with four wins and four second places. In 1995 Owen competed in five F3 races for Alan Docking Racing and won the International F3 Cup at Donington.

Hired by RouseSport to partner Gary Ayles in the Nissan Primeras for 1996, Owen had something of a torrid season, usually finishing among the tail-enders.

Race History

Born: 9 November 1953, Dumfries
Lives: Banbury

1969: 1st, Scottish Kart Championship
1977: 1st, BARC Formula Ford Championship
1979: 1st, Shellsport Martini FF2000
Championship
1987: 2nd, World Sportscar Championship, C2 Class (Ecosse)
1988: 2nd, Thundersaloons Championship
1996: 4th, BTCC (Honda Accord)
1997: BTCC (Nissan Primera)

Race History

Born: 5 October 1973, Belfast
Lives: Comber, Northern Ireland

1989: 1st, Northern Ireland and All Ireland Junior Britain Kart Championship
1990: 1st, Northern Ireland 100 National
Kart Championship
1992: 4th, Northern Ireland Formula Ford 1600 Championship
1994: 1st, Formula Vauxhall-Lotus Championship
1995: 1st, International Formula 3 Cup
1996: BTCC (Nissan Primera)

Alain Menu

Twice runner up in the BTCC, Alain Menu began his career at the Ecole Elf Winfield in 1984.

Transferring to Britain in 1987, he was second in the Esso Formula Ford Championship. He upgraded to Formula 3 in 1988 but the bigger F3000 cars beckoned, and Alain competed in five races on the F3000 circuit in 1991. In 1992 he drove a Prodrive M3 in the BTCC and he joined the Renault works team for the 1993 BTCC. Racing for Renault in France, Menu suffered a broken leg, but he was back on his feet to debut the new Laguna in the 1994 BTCC. Two wins, three seconds and five thirds gave him second in the Championship.

For 1995, the cars were run by Williams Renault Dealer Racing, and with new team-mate Will Hoy, Menu re-established his credentials with seven victories, three seconds, three thirds and six pole positions, to come second overall in the Drivers' Championship. Will Hoy's efforts combined to give Renault the Manufacturers' title.

In 1996 Menu continued to set about the opposition with a vengeance. Alain has always looked a potential BTCC champion, and by mid-'97 was set for the title.

Race History

Born: 9 August 1963, Geneva, Switzerland

Lives: Geneva and Warwickshire

1984: 2nd, Elf Winfield School, Paul Ricard

1987: 2nd, Esso Formula Ford Championship

1990: 2nd, British F3000 Championship

1994: 2nd, BTCC (Renault Laguna)

1995: 2nd, BTCC (Renault Laguna)

1996: 2nd, BTCC (Renault Laguna)

1997: BTCC (Laguna)

Matt Neal

Matthew Neal began racing saloons in 1988, and came second in the Brands Hatch winter series with a Fiesta. He won his class in the BTCC in 1990 with a BMW M3 and in 1991 Matt drove a Nissan Skyline GT-R in Class A in the BTCC and won that, taking the Silverstone 500km (310 miles) honours along the way.

In 1993 he won the Total Cup section of the BTCC with a BMW 318i, and moved on to a Mazda Xedos for 1994. It was not such a good season, terminating in a seriously spectacular high-speed roll at Silverstone, and Mazda pulled out soon afterwards. In 1995, Matt tackled the Total Cup with a Mondeo. Everything came good and he won the privateers' category from Richard Kaye and Nigel Smith, coming 21st overall in the BTCC tables.

Matt's Mondeo is prepared and run by Team Dynamics, which is owned by his father Steve Neal, who was himself a legend in the late 1960s and early-1970s. For 1996 he was teamed with 1990 BTCC champion Robb Gravett, and after ironing out problems with the Mondeo's suspension pick-up points, the 1997 season saw some improvement.

Race History

Born: 20 December 1966, Birmingham

Lives: Stourbridge

1989: 4th, Ford Credit Fiesta Championship

1990: 1st, BTCC Class B (BMW M3); 1st, Willhire 24-Hours; 1st, Silverstone 500km

1991: 1st, BTCC Class A (Nissan Skyline); 1st, Silverstone 500km

1993: 1st, BTCC Total Cup (BMW 318i)

1995: 1st, BTCC Total Cup (Ford Mondeo)

1996: 3rd, BTCC Total Cup (Ford Mondeo)

1997: BTCC Total Cup (Ford Mondeo)

Tiff Needell

Tiff caught the public eye as, arguably, the best presenter on BBC TV's *Top Gear*, but he was a motor sporting personality long before that. In the early 1970s he was a rising star in Formula Ford. By 1975 Tiff had won the Townsend Thoresen Formula Ford Championship, and went on to contest the British Formula 3 series for the next three seasons with a Safir-Toyota and a March-Triumph.

There was a single F1 drive for Ensign in 1980, and thereafter Tiff's career took him into the world of Group C sports racing cars. Between 1981 and 1992 he drove for Aston Martin, Dome, Porsche and Spice in World Sportscar Championship events.

It was no surprise to find a driver as versatile as Tiff in touring cars, and he took a win in the 1989 BTCC with an RS500 Cosworth. In 1992 he was a member of the Nissan team, placing seventh in the BTCC with a Primera. He drove for both Vauxhall and Nissan in 1993, concentrating on the Primera for the 1994 season. Things wound down in 1995, Tiff participating in a medley of races, often for the benefit of *Top Gear*.

Race History

Born: 29 October 1951, Havant, Hampshire	(Ensign) **1984:** 8th, Le Mans 24-Hours (Kremer Porsche 956)
1975: 1st, Townsend Thoresen Formula Ford Championship	**1986:** 9th, Shell Gemini 1000, Brands Hatch (March-Porsche)
1978: 4th, British Formula 3 Championship	**1992:** 7th, BTCC (Nissan Primera)
1980: Formula 1 World Championship	**1996:** 19th, Le Mans 24-Hours (Lister Storm)

Kieth O'dor

Kieth ranked as one of the hardest triers and one of the most unlucky of BTCC participants, where to an extent he was an under-rated talent. He came to prominence with the backing of his father Jan Odor's celebrated Janspeed performance-tuning company, but his talent was sufficient to stand him on his own merits. His most prominent victory was his BTCC win with the Primera at Silverstone in July 1993.

In 1995 Kieth competed in the German Superturenwagen Cup, with Nissan team-mates Ivan Capelli and Sascha Maasen. Kieth had just won Nissan's first German Super Touring race from pole position at the daunting Avus street circuit in Berlin – two long parallel straights, two huge loops at either end – and was running in the second race when tragedy struck. The Primera was T-boned at high speed when Kieth was involved in a mid-race incident, and he didn't have much of a chance.

His untimely death was a great loss to motor racing, and ironically it was in a category of the sport which has a remarkably good record for safety.

Race History

Born: 5 April 1962, Salisbury	Championship (Ford Sierra RS)
Died: 11 September 1995, Berlin	**1990:** 1st, British Group N Championship (Nissan Skyline)
1987: 1st, British Saloon Car Championship 2000cc class (Peugeot 205)	**1993:** 6th, BTCC (Nissan Primera)
1989: 1st, British Production Saloons	**1995:** 10th, German ADAC Super Touring series (Nissan Primera)

Paul Radisich

Paul's career took off in 1983 with the New Zealand's Bruce McLaren 'Most Likely to Succeed' award. In 1984 Paul won the 'Driver to Europe' award, following in the footsteps of greats like Bruce McLaren and Denny Hulme, and spent two seasons in Formula 3.

Back in New Zealand he won the prestigious Lady Wigram Trophy, before moving to the USA to contest the 1987 SuperVee Championship. Over the summer period 'down under', Paul took the honours in New Zealand's Formule Libre series and won the Denny Hulme Trophy.

Highlights for 1988 included five wins in the US SuperVee series, winning him the Championship and he also won the Australian Formula 2 Grand Prix. His first real taste of Touring Car racing earned him second place in a Class 2 BMW M3 at the Bathurst 1000. The following year he teamed with the legendary Peter Brock to race a Sierra RS500 to victory in the New Zealand Endurance racing series.

The personable Kiwi deserved better luck than was possible with the '96 Mondeo.

Race History

Born: 9 October 1962, Auckland, New Zealand	**1989:** 1st, New Zealand Endurance series (Ford Sierra Cosworth RS500)
Lives: Leamington Spa	**1993:** 1st, FIA Touring Car World Cup, BTCC (Ford Mondeo)
1984: Formula 3, New Zealand's Driver to Europe award	**1994:** 3rd, BTCC
1988: 1st, Australian Formula 2 Grand Prix	**1995:** 6th, BTCC (Ford Mondeo)
	1997: BTCC (Mondeo)

For the 1990 Bathurst classic, Paul was teamed up with Jeff Allam, and they came second in a Sierra RS500. In 1992 he won the Fuji 500 round of the Japanese Touring Car Championship in a BMW M3. Team Mondeo and the BTCC beckoned, and Paul took third place in the Championship. He also did brilliantly to win the inaugural FIA World Touring Car Cup at Monza. A full BTCC season in the Mondeo earned him just two wins – although at one point he had seemed the most likely person to challenge and beat Tarquini's Alfa – and again he ended the year in third place.

Alas, the Mondeos were slipping further out of contention, and there was just one win at Silverstone in 1995. The new-for-1997 Mondeos would hopefully bring the personable Kiwi more success.

Roberto Ravaglia

An engineer by trade, Roberto Ravaglia got into motor sport with karts. He was twice winner of the Italian Kart Championship between 1974 and 1979. His racing extended to that traditional proving ground for racers destined for the top, the European F3 circuit in 1982 and 1983, running a Dallara and a Ralt.

He made the transition to saloon cars in 1984 with a BMW 635CSi, and in the two seasons that followed he enjoyed two race wins in the European Touring Car Championship. It would all come together for Roberto in 1986, when he captured the European title with the 635CSi. In 1988 he took the German national championship in an M3. Roberto returned to Italy with the M3 in 1990, and for the next three years he was the Italian Touring Car Champion.

The 1993 title was won with the 318i, which he campaigned with again in 1994. His main opponent in the inaugural German series, in 1995, was Frank Biela in the Audi when he drove a BMW 320i. For 1996 and the BTCC, Roberto was reunited with Schnitzer, having been in the Italian CiBiEmme and Bigazzi teams.

Steve Robertson

Steve came to the BTCC in 1996 after a promising career in single-seaters rather petered out, and his chief role was number two to Paul Radisich at Team Mondeo. His finishing record was good, but it was his lot to run with the tail-enders, and he ended 1996 with just two points.

His career in motor racing got going in 1985 when he won sixth place in the Dunlop-Autosport sponsored 'Star of Tomorrow' competition and he became British FF2000 Champion in 1988. Graduating to Formula 3, Steve won first time out at Donington and came third in the 1989 and 1990 Championships.

Steve moved up a class to drive in six European F3000 races in 1992 in a Reynard-Ford, but retired mid-season through illness. Over in the USA the following year for the Indy Lights series, Steve won the 'Rookie of the Year' award. He became the first ever British winner of the series in 1994, with four wins from 11 races. And there, surprisingly, his run of success in single-seaters ended. It was, however, a promising enough CV to land the Mondeo drive.

Race History

Born: 26 May 1957, Mestre, Venice

Lives: Mestre

1974: 1st, Italian Kart Championship
1986: 1st, European Touring Car Championship (BMW 635CSi)
1987: 1st, World Touring Car Championship

(BMW M3)
1989: 1st, German Touring Car Championship (BMW M3)
1994: 1st, Spa-Francorchamps 24-Hours (BMW 318is)
1995: 1st, Nürburgring 24-Hours (BMW 320i)
1996: BTCC (BMW 320i)

Race History

Born: 4 July 1965, London

Lives: Hertfordshire

1985: 6th, Dunlop-Autosport 'Star of Tomorrow' contest; 8th, Formula Ford 1600 Championship
1986: 4th, RAC Formula Ford

Championship
1988: 1st, Formula Ford 2000 Championship
1989: 5th, British Formula 3 Championship
1994: 1st, US Indy Lights series
1996: BTCC (Ford Mondeo)

Andy Rouse

Team principal of RouseSport, Andy Rouse retired from active race participation at the end of 1995 with over 60 touring car wins to his credit – more than any other driver. The four-times British Saloon Car Champion's career spanned more than three decades and in the mid-1980s Rouse built a hugely successful race preparation and development business on the strength of his race wins.

In 1993 RouseSport was engaged to develop and race the works Mondeos, and Rouse and Radisich enjoyed a string of high placings the following season.

After Rouse hung up his helmet in 1995, the Mondeo failed to match up to expectations. In 1996 RouseSport prepared and ran the Nissan Primeras.

A keen advocate of safety first, Rouse insists that behaviour on the road requires a totally different approach to that required for racing. 'Driving on the road is a bigger responsibility than most people realise. Driver education is pathetically lax,' he says. 'There should be a 'P' plate which you get when you pass your test, and a limit of 60mph.'

Rickard Rydell

Rickard Rydell had a promising career in single-seaters, which began in karts. He was Swedish National 100cc Kart Champion in 1984 and 1985, graduating straight to Formula 3 in 1986. The following two years he was runner-up in the Swedish F3 series, coming to Britain in 1989 to drive for Eddie Jordan in Formula 3. Rickard had one race victory, at Thruxton – and if you can win there you must be good – and finished the season in fourth place.

Driving for AJS in F3000, Rydell obtained a win at Brands Hatch in 1990, and came fourth in the series. He returned to the British Formula 3 scene in 1991 and competed in the World Cup races in Macau and in Fuji. For 1992 he stayed with TOM'S Toyota in Japan, and as a regular frontrunner he won the Macau F3 Grand Prix, setting fastest lap on the way. He was third overall in the 1992 championship and second in 1993.

There was a major change in Rydell's career in 1994, when he was invited by TWR to drive the new Volvo 850 Estate in the BTCC, alongside Jan Lammers. It was a steep learning curve and the car was more frequently

Race History

Born: 2 December 1947
Lives: Radford Semele, Warwickshire

1975: 1st, BTCC (Dolomite Sprint)
1983: 1st, BTCC (Alfa Romeo GTV6)
1984: 1st, BTCC (Rover SD1)

1985: 1st, BTCC (Ford Sierra)
1988: 1st, Tourist Trophy (RS500)
1993: RouseSport develops Ford Mondeo for BTCC
1996: RouseSport develops Nissan Primera for BTCC

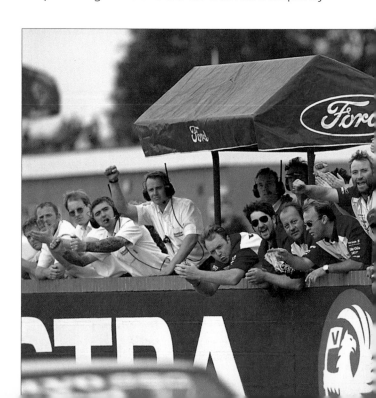

Race History

Born: 22 September 1967, Stockholm, Sweden	(Reynard-Cosworth) **1992:** 3rd, Japanese Formula 3 series
Lives: Stockholm	**1994:** 14th, BTCC (Volvo 850 Estate)
1984: 1st, Swedish Kart Championship	**1995:** 3rd, BTCC (Volvo 850)
1989: 3rd, British F3 Championship	**1996:** 3rd, BTCC (Volvo 850)
1990: 4th, British F3000 Championship	**1997:** BTCC (Volvo S40)

Giampiero Simoni

Giampiero Simoni was a top-notch kartist, winning the 135cc World Championship in 1988. The personable Italian came to Britain in 1989 to contest the Formula Ford 1600 series with a works Van Diemen, and came a creditable seventh overall. Back in Italy, he drove for three seasons in the National F3 Championship, winning once with his Dallara-Alfa. At the end of 1992 Giampiero moved up to F3000, and spent the next full season with Mythos driving a Reynard-Judd.

Hired by Alfa Corse for the assault on the BTCC with the Alfa 155TS, he spent 1994 very much in a supporting role to Gabriele Tarquini, but was on occasion just as quick and won the final round, further consolidating Alfa's dominance in the Championship. Giampiero was fifth in the final points standings, but in 1995 the cars were off the pace, and his best result was a fifth. By mid-season Tarquini had been drafted back into the Prodrive-run operation in a vain bid for points, and Simoni was undeservedly despatched to race the 155 in the Spanish Super Touring series. His half season in the 1995 BTCC netted enough points for 15th place.

on the pace in 1995, and with Tim Harvey as teammate, Rickard scored four race wins and took an amazing 13 pole positions – which in mid-1996 still stood as a record. He didn't handle the start too well, and was swamped by the pack. However, his results were good enough for third in the BTCC points tables.

In 1996 the Volvos of Rydell and Burt were soon snapping at the heels of the Audis, and the Super Swede narrowly missed being runner-up in the 1996 series, although Volvo pipped Renault for the Manufacturers' prize. He looked best placed to catch the Lagunas in 1997.

Members of the TWR Volvo pit-crew applaud another 850 victory.

Race History

Born: 12 June 1969, Milan	**1990:** European F3000 Championship (Mythos Reynard)
Lives: Porto san Giorgio	**1993:** Super Touring Championship (Alfa Romeo)
1988: 1st, World Kart Championship, 135cc	**1994:** 5th, BTCC (Alfa Romeo)
1989: 7th, British Formula Ford 1600 Championship (Van Diemen)	**1995:** 15th, BTCC (Alfa Romeo)

Touring Cars

Nigel Smith

Nigel was the manufacturer of John Player Special merchandise and apparel for Team Lotus during the 1970s and was a regular top five runner on the European karting circuit.

He ran in F3 before graduating to F3000 in 1993. Smith drove his Reynard 92D-Tickford DFY in the British series and was a top three finisher in over half the races. He also drove in the 1995 South African F3000 Grand Prix at Kyalami, but retired. His best drive in F3000 was in the Boss Formula race at Thruxton in June 1996, which he won by 12 seconds at an average 192km/h (120mph). In that race he had faced some F1 machinery, including a pair of Footwork-Judds.

Nigel was a consistent runner in the BTCC in 1994 and 1995, and his modest placings were the legacy of a privateer's restricted budget.

Sponsorship for his ex-Ray Mallock Vauxhall Cavalier came from HMSO Bookshops, and he used it to good advantage to come third in the privateers' Total Cup in 1995. In 1996 Smith raced in the Scandinavian Nordic Touring Car Championship.

Steve Soper

Now a veteran, Soper is still a key player on the international stage, having competed successfully in Japan and Europe. He began winning in Mini Coopers, taking the British trophy twice, in 1977 and 1979. He also drove the Radbourne Fiat X1/9, and then the Fiesta Cup was his in 1980. He won the RAC Tourist Trophy in 1983 in a TWR Rover SD1, and should have been BTCC Champion but for legal wrangles over the car's engine.

In 1988 he was second in the European series, having won six races with the Cossie. Between 1989 and 1992 Steve raced in Germany, scoring nine wins in the German Touring Car programme with the Zakspeed and Bigazzi teams' BMW M3s. Amongst these was the Spa 24-Hours of 1992. He was second in the BTCC in 1993 with three victories in the BMW 318i but there was only one BTCC race win in 1994.

The following year was a good one for Soper. He became Japanese Touring Car Champion as well as winning the Spa 24-Hours and coming third in the Touring Car World Cup event at Paul Ricard. He took part in the German series in 1996.

Race History

Born: 17 March 1951, Surbiton
Lives: Chippenham, Wiltshire

1979: 1st, Belgian, Dutch, New Zealand Superkart Grands Prix
1984: 1st, TV Times Superkart series
1993: 4th, Moosehead GP, Canada; British F3000 Championship (Reynard 92D)
1994: BTCC Total Cup (Vauxhall Cavalier)
1995: 3rd, BTCC Total Cup (Vauxhall Cavalier)
1996: 1st, Boss F3000 race, Thruxton, (Reynard)

Race History

Born: 27 September 1952, Greenford
Lives: Monaco

1977: 1st, Mini Cooper Cup
1983: 1st, Tourist Trophy (Rover Vitesse)
1992: 1st, Spa-Francorchamps 24-Hours (BMW M3)
1993: 2nd, BTCC (BMW 318i)
1995: 1st, Japanese Touring Car Championship; 1st Spa-Francorchamps 24-Hours
1996: German Superturenwagen Championship (BMW 320i)

Gabriele Tarquini

Best known for his domination of the 1994 BTCC, Gabriele had previously enjoyed a lengthy career in single-seaters. He drove an F3000 March-Cosworth in 1985 and made his Formula 1 debut in 1987 with Osella-Alfa Romeo. In 1988 he drove for Coloni and in 1989 for AGS and Fondmetal. Tarquini also had one win in the Italian Touring Car series with a BMW M3.

Tarquini abandoned these struggling F1 teams for the more robust world of Touring Cars. Under Alfa's wing for 1993 he drove a 155 TS and as Alfa Corse turned its attentions to the BTCC for 1994, Gabriele set about the rout which began at Thruxton, and, brushing aside the protests about aerodynamic anomalies and a horrifying barrel roll at Knockhill, ended with a title-clinching double header at Silverstone in the Grand Prix meeting. Eight victories and some high placings were good

Race History

Born: 2 March 1962, Giulianova, Italy
Lives: Giulianova

1984: 1st, World 125cc Kart Championship
1992: 5th, Italian Superturismo Championship (BMW)
1993: 3rd, Italian Superturismo Championship (Alfa Romeo 155)
1994: 1st, BTCC (Alfa Romeo 155)
1995: 7th, Italian Superturismo Championship; 16th, BTCC (Alfa Romeo 155)
1997: BTCC (Honda Accord)

enough for the Championship. Gabriele was despatched to race Alfas in the German and Italian Championships in 1995, but he was brought back into the BTCC squad in mid-season.

Gabriele went off to the Class 1 International Touring Car Championship, taking a well-earned win at Silverstone. For 1997 he was back in the BTCC, doing well for Honda.

In early 1995, Alfa's hopes rested on Simoni – seen here kerb-hopping at Donington – and Warwick.

James Thompson

In May 1995, less than two weeks after his 21st birthday, James became the BTCC's youngest race winner. In a sport ruled by experienced talents, a breakthrough such as his is rare. It was cut sadly short by a 200km/h (125mph) crash testing the Cavalier at Knockhill. James missed out on the Championship's 10 final rounds but still finished seventh overall in the series.

The son of David Thompson, a well-known rallyist, James won the Senior British 100cc Short Circuit Championship in 1990, moving into single-seaters in 1991. In 1993 he drove one of six Honda Civic V-Tecs in the Castrol-sponsored scholarship and from 13 races he won seven times, scored four further podium finishes, and set nine pole position ties and eight fastest laps. Not surprisingly, he took the National Saloon Car Cup.

In his BTCC debut season, James raced in the Total Cup category with a Peugeot 405 Mi16. At 19, he was the Championship's youngest competitor. Driving the Vectra in 1996, he gave the car its maiden victory, at Snetterton in round 11. At Honda for 1997, James put in some strong performances.

Race History

Born: 26 April 1974, York
Lives: York

1990: 1st, Senior British 100cc Kart Champion, Winter series
1992: 4th, Formula Vauxhall Junior Championship
1993: 1st, National Saloon Car Cup (Honda Civic)
1995: 7th, BTCC (Vauxhall Cavalier)
1996: 10th, BTCC (Vauxhall Vectra)
1997: BTCC (Honda Accord)

Derek Warwick

The biggest name to be linked with the BTCC in recent years – apart from Nigel Mansell's one-off TOCA outing at Donington – Derek Warwick came to Alfa Romeo with high hopes for the 1995 season. Outclassed though the team was, Derek was clearly struggling to apply his Formula 1 skills to the particular front-drive requirements of touring cars.

Derek was European Formula Ford Champion in 1976, and started to hit the big time in 1978 when he was British F3 Champion. In 1980 he was second in the European F2 Championship with the Toleman Hart.

A veteran of 147 Grands Prix, Derek's best year in F1 was 1984 when he scored three second places for Renault. Derek was second in the World Sportscar series for Jaguar in 1986. He took the title for Peugeot in 1992, and won that year's Le Mans 24-Hours.

His best result in the Alfa 155 was eighth, and he was 19th in the 1995 points standings. In 1996 he drove a Courage-Porsche into 13th place at Le Mans with Mario Andretti and Jan Lammers. Derek partnered John Cleland in the BTCC Vectra squad in 1997.

Race History

Born: 27 August 1954 Alresford, Hampshire
Lives: St John, Jersey

1976: 1st, European Formula Ford 1600 Championship
1981: Joined Toleman F1 team
1984 3rd, Belgian, British, South African Grands Prix (Renault)
1992: 1st, World Sportscar Championship (Peugeot)
1995: 19th, BTCC (Alfa Romeo)
1996: 13th, Le Mans 24-Hours (Courage-Porsche)
1997: BTCC (Vauxhall Vectra)

Patrick Watts

Patrick's early days in motor sport were in 850 Minis, and he was national champion in 1979. In the next three seasons he campaigned a variety of touring cars in UK Production Saloon events, including an Escort RS Turbo and Saab 900 Turbo. He was also runner-up in the MG Metro Challenge and BL 1275GT series in 1980, 1981 and 1982.

In the 1983 and 1984 seasons he contested the British and European Touring Car Championships as a works driver in the Rover Metro team. Patrick was a leading contender in the Uno Turbo series in 1986, particularly in the wet.

In 1988 he became the first champion of the inaugural Honda CRX one-make series, and took the title again in 1990. He was also Mazda MX5 champ that year, proving that he had the ability to handle rear-drive cars with equal aplomb.

Race History

Born: 21 November 1955, Farnborough, Kent

Lives: Marden, Kent

1979: 1st, National Mini 850 Championship

1988: 1st, Honda CRX Championship

1990: 1st, Honda CRX Championship; 1st Mazda MX5 Championship

1991: Esso Production Saloon Car Championship (Peugeot 309 GTi)

1996: 16th, BTCC (Peugeot 406)

1997: BTCC (Peugeot 406)

More recently, Patrick has been associated with Peugeot, driving a 309GTi to victory in the Group N category of the BTCC in 1991. He drove a Mazda Xedos in 1992 and 1993, switching to the Peugeot 405 for 1994 and 1995. In the new Total Team Peugeot 406 for 1996, Patrick continued to show the form that characterized his BTCC performances. In 1997 he was a typically determined mid-field runner.

Despite vast experience in saloons, Watts couldn't make an impression with the 406 in 1996.

Jo Winkelhock

Smokin' Jo, hardly ever seen without a lit cigarette, is a natural Touring Car racer. Coming from a motor racing family – his late brother Manfred was a Formula 1 and World Sportscar Championship contender – Jo had been a significant player on the German domestic scene since the mid-1980s. He then came to prominence in Britain with his convincing victory in the 1993 BTCC in a BMW 320i.

In Germany, Jo won the Porsche 944 Turbo Cup series in 1986. He won the German Formula 3 Championship with a Reynard-VW in 1988 and in 1990 won the Nürburgring 24-Hours Touring Car event in a BMW M3. He did so again in 1991 in a Schnitzer M3.

Jo Winkelhock's BMW team-mate for the BTCC in 1996 was Touring Car expert Roberto Ravaglia.

Race History

Born: 24 October 1960, Waiblingen
Lives: Waiblingen

1986: 1st, Porsche Turbo Cup series
1988: 1st, German Formula 3 Championship (Reynard VW)
1990: 1st, Nürburgring 24-Hours

(BMW M3)
1991: 1st, Nürburgring 24-Hours (BMW M3)
1993: 1st, BTCC (BMW 318i)
1994: 1st, Asia-Pacific Touring Car series (BMW 318i)
1996: BTCC (BMW 320i)

His five wins in the 1993 BTCC, when he drove a BMW 318i, made him a favourite for title honours in 1994, but Alfa and Tarquini upset the form book.

In 1995 Jo mounted an assault on the ADAC German Super Touring Championship, which he took for BMW from Audi's Frank Biela. Back in Britain for 1996, Winkelhock headed straight into a potential confrontation with his German adversary Biela. But the four-wheel-drive Audis were more than a match for the rear-drive BMWs.

Appendices

The roll of honour for the British Touring Car Championship serves as a concise guide to the greatest drivers in Touring Car racing. The winning cars show that racing is episodic, with one make dominant for two or more seasons at a time.

BTCC CHAMPIONS 1958-1996

YEAR	DRIVER	CAR	YEAR	DRIVER	CAR
1958	Jack Sears	Austin A105	1978	Richard Longman	Mini 1275GT
1959	Jeff Uren	Ford Zephyr	1979	Richard Longman	Mini 1275GT
1960	Doc Shepherd	Austin A40	1980	Win Percy	Mazda RX7
1961	John Whitmore	Mini	1981	Win Percy	Mazda RX7
1962	John Love	Mini Cooper	1982	Win Percy	Toyota Celica
1963	Jack Sears	Ford Galaxie	1983	Andy Rouse	Alfa Romeo GTV6
1964	Jim Clark	Lotus Cortina	1984	Andy Rouse	Rover Vitesse
1965	Roy Pierpoint	Ford Mustang	1985	Andy Rouse	Ford Sierra Cosworth Turbo
1966	John Fitzpatrick	Ford Anglia	1986	Chris Hodgetts	Toyota Corolla
1967	Frank Gardner	Ford Falcon	1987	Chris Hodgetts	Toyota Corolla
1968	Frank Gardner	Ford Cortina-Lotus/Ford Escort	1988	Frank Sytner	BMW M3
1969	Alec Poole	Mini Cooper S	1989	John Cleland	Vauxhall Astra GTE
1970	Bill McGovern	Sunbeam Imp	1990	Robb Gravett	Ford Sierra Cosworth RS500
1971	Bill McGovern	Sunbeam Imp	1991	Will Hoy	BMW M3
1972	Bill McGovern	Sunbeam Imp	1992	Tim Harvey	BMW 318is
1973	Frank Gardner	Chevrolet Camaro	1993	Jo Winkelhock	BMW 318i
1974	Bernard Unett	Hillman Avenger	1994	Gabriele Tarquini	Alfa Romeo 155
1975	Andy Rouse	Triumph Dolomite Sprint	1995	John Cleland	Vauxhall Cavalier
1976	Bernard Unett	Chrysler Avenger GT	1996	Frank Biela	Audi Quattro
1977	Bernard Unett	Chrysler Avenger GT			

Index